The Healing Crystal

To Mrs. Phillips,
with many crystalline thoughts
and blessings.

Geoffrey Keyte

16th August 1989

The Healing Crystal

A Practical Handbook

Geoffrey Keyte

BLANDFORD

Blandford Press, An imprint of Cassell
Artillery House, Artillery Row
London SW1P 1RT

Copyright © Crystal Research Foundation 1989

First published 1989

Distributed in the United States by
Sterling Publishing Co., Inc.
2 Park Avenue, New York, NY 10016

Distributed in Australia by
Capricorn Link (Australia) Pty Ltd
PO Box 665, Lane Cove, NSW 2066

British Library Cataloguing in Publication Data

Keyte, Geoffrey
  The healing crystal: a discovery handbook.
  1. Crystals. Occult aspects.
  I. Title
  133

ISBN 0–7137–2099–9 (Paperback)

Typeset by Inforum Typesetting, Portsmouth
Printed and bound in Great Britain by Biddles Ltd, Guildford
and Kings Lynn

This book is lovingly dedicated to my wife, Judith, without whose support I could not have written it.

Contents

Acknowledgements

The preparation of this book involved the help of many persons who have been involved with crystal healing therapy — both as part of the Crystal Research Foundation and elsewhere — all over the world.

Thanks are also due to Ya 'Acov Mikk Khan for the photography, to the long list of healers, therapists and suppliers who have allowed their names to be listed, and to Beryl Roberts, Gillian Collins, Kushal Gupta and others for inclusion of case histories.

Preface

From my experience and personal philosophy, I would submit that all knowledge is to be found within the Higher Cosmic Consciousness. My own interpretation of our consciousness is that everything that exists has been known since time first began, since our planet was first created. There is nothing new, only rediscovery. I believe firmly in the existence of the ancient continent of Atlantis and its knowledge where the use of crystals and gemstones pre-dated allopathic medicine. It is said that in the days of Atlantis, Lemuria and beyond, crystals would have been the only means by which healing would have taken place.

Technologically, our world has travelled far since those days. We have had many opportunities to learn from the harsh realities of the cataclysmic destruction of Atlantis. Will we never learn? As it was then, so it could be today!

The truth is very simple and it seems to me that the human race — all civilisation as we know it today — East and West — has lost its way Progress has become minimal, in some cases even retrogressive! This book is all about my perception of the truth. Many of you reading this book may be old Atlantean souls. Maybe some of you will even be able to remember a few details of your incarnations in Atlantis. You will find that it becomes more and more natural for you to use crystals in your everyday life.

The knowledge and experiences included here will help to reawaken your own inner being and expand your crystal consciousness. Once again you will be able to establish complete rapport and harmony with the crystal kingdom. You will be able to use the immense knowledge that crystals bring you for the benefit of every-one who travels across your pathway of life.

This book is written in the belief and hope that it will touch your heart and mind; that it will enable you to achieve a greater under-standing of the world in which you live and that you will be able to allow the purity of crystal energy to enter your heart and life.

My door is always open and if you feel moved to write a few words to me — and perhaps share with me your own experiences of using crystals — then I shall always be delighted to hear from you.

With all crystal blessings,
GEOFFREY KEYTE
St Annes-on-Sea
Lancashire, England

Crystals through the Ages

Crystals and gemstones have intrigued human beings since the very beginning of time itself. The first recorded gemstones were amethyst, quartz and rock crystals, garnet, jade, jasper, lapis lazuli, pearl, emerald and turquoise. People have, it seems, always known (perhaps intuitively in the first instance) that certain crystals and gemstones possess therapeutic healing properties.

The term 'natural health' in today's terminology is usually taken to mean the major therapies of acupuncture, osteopathy, homoeopathy, herbalism, massage and hypnotherapy. Crystal healing is still regarded by many people as a 'fringe' therapy. But crystal healing is by no means 'new'. In Atlantis, the use of quartz crystals in the treatment of *all* health conditions would have been considered in preference to any other allopathic medicine that might have been available at the same time. The use of crystals for healing purposes has been practised by many different cultures and religions throughout the world since the days of Atlantis. Today, therefore, we are only reintroducing and rediscovering techniques that were used successfully in the treatment of all health conditions before our own Western civilisation came into existence.

The Chinese, for example, have used jade in the treatment of kidney and bladder problems for a period in excess of 5000 years.

Lapis lazuli, carnelian, amber, turquoise, jade, tiger's eye, serpentine and chrysoberyl were just some of the stones that were discovered in Egyptian tombs. Jade was one of the most common gemstones in the time of ancient Egypt and was often used in their trade and commerce as a means of barter.

Atlantis

Atlantis, according to Plato, was a very large continent stretching from what is now the east coast of America to where Greece is today. In Plato's book *Critias* he describes Atlantis, which apparently was once known as Poseidon. In his book Plato observes that the high point of the Atlantean civilisation occurred when gods walked with men. I believe that there were many very large crystals in Atlantis possessing an extremely high-energy 'voltage' which the Atlanteans were able to channel for a wide variety of purposes.

Besides using crystals for healing purposes, the Atlanteans probably would have used crystals as their primary source of power and energy — a power and energy that could produce 'electricity' for lighting, computers and many other mechanical innovations. They may even have had their own vehicular transport. It seems that their crystal power was even greater than our twentieth-century nuclear energy!

From my own personal research and experiences I have discovered that even some of my very small quartz crystals possess a significant amount of electrical energy and power. And it is this very energy, of course, that I am able to use in my own crystal healing treatment sessions in my clinic. Having thus seen and experienced the concentrated level of crystal energy and power that is present in fairly small quartz crystals, one can only wonder at the thought of how much crystal energy and power would be available to us if we had the opportunity of tapping into an enormous quartz crystal, perhaps a million times the size of the average small crystal. It is quite beyond the capacity of the human mind to actually visualise and appreciate the amount of constant power and energy that we would have at our disposal!

However, this is a very simplistic description of the true situation as there are several other important factors involved. The priests and priestesses of Atlantis apparently knew a great deal more than we will ever know — despite our so-called high-tech civilisation — about the natural laws of our world and universe. For one thing, they seemed to be able to communicate with each other very effectively by telepathy. They knew how to harness the power of the mind. Most of the crystal power that existed in Atlantis appears to have been activated through mental contact and communication. The Atlanteans were able to closely attune themselves to the vibrational structure of each individual crystal — whether large or small — and this resulted in them being able to channel and direct the crystal energy towards whichever function it was to be used for.

One of the prime sources of information relating to Atlantis and its crystal healing techniques is Dr Frank Alper, founder of the Arizona Metaphysical Society. Frank has written a trilogy of books entitled *Exploring Atlantis*, and many of the crystal healing books that have been written during the past few years have based their ideas and thoughts on information to be found in Frank's excellent books. The following description of the Healing Temple comes from *Exploring Atlantis* Vol 1.

Most of the healing work done in Atlantis centred around the great Healing Temple, which was a very large building, constructed from a marble-like building material. As one approached the Temple there was a flight of twelve steps at the main entrance. On reaching the top step, one walked between twelve columns, six on each side, to enter the Temple.

The Temple needed no doors as it was never closed. It was always available to everyone whatever the time, day or night. Upon entering through the arches one would find oneself inside a huge circular room some 14 metres (45 feet) in diameter. This was the main central hall of healing. In the middle of the room was a table, which was 3 metres (9 feet) long and 1 metre (3 feet) wide. The top of the table was constructed of a grid made of a metallic alloy called 'orlax', containing silver, ground crystal dust and copper. The table was supported by a pedestal shaped like a pyramid and made of crystal.

Around the entire circumference of the room were cubicles which contained individual healing chambers. The ceiling of the room was domed and composed of interlocking crystals in various colours, which formed patterns of ancient symbols. Some were in the form of hieroglyphics. Behind the circular room, on either side, were individual rooms for study, meditation and healings of a specialised nature.

The cubicles — or individual healing chambers — would have

been used for many purposes. For example, pregnant women were placed in cubicles shortly after conception and sealed in the cubicle by a wall of crystal. The crystals were then 'energised' by a method similar to laser treatment, in varying frequencies and colours of energy. This was to ensure the woman's health, to implant certain desired vibrations within the foetus and to set the conditions for the child's incarnation. The women remained in these cubicles for a period of 24 hours.

The cubicles would also have been used, from time to time, by those who wanted to accelerate their rate of development and to elevate the levels of their vibration frequencies by exposure to higher and higher levels of crystal energy.

The healing table in the great chamber was used for very specific functions. When the time had come for an individual to die, whether it was through the normal ageing process or from an advanced disease, the soul was assisted in making the transition rapidly and without hesitation. This was accomplished by exposing the individual to certain rays of energy. Such assistance was not considered to be interfering with the normal process of life but was seen as quite necessary. It was understood that when individuals passed on they would be reincarnated almost immediately in order to continue their work. This made it essential that they enjoyed a peaceful and harmonious transition. There was no time for souls to linger.

The final destruction of Atlantis was brought about because many of the priests became corrupt and wanted to use the crystals for their own evil purposes; enslaving their fellow men and gaining complete control of their minds and bodies. Their misuse of the crystals was so totally contrary to all the natural laws of the universe that the crystal energy vibrations became unstable and finally resulted in tremendous cataclysmic explosions and flooding — and Atlantis slid slowly beneath the sea and was gone forever.

Not everyone, however, perished in the final annihilation: some of the priests who had not become corrupted knew, well in advance, that Atlantis was to be destroyed and also the exact date on which this was to occur. Thus certain priests and priestesses escaped from Atlantis and were transported to various parts of the world where their task was to make a new life for themselves and to found a new civilisation. Some went to South America, some to Israel and some to Egypt.

Egypt

The Atlanteans who settled in Egypt brought with them much of their knowledge and ideas. It must be remembered, however, that the earth vibrations existing in the land of Egypt were on a different wavelength from those which existed in Atlantis and therefore it was not possible to reproduce and reintroduce all the technology that they knew from their days in Atlantis. They were, though, able to use their crystal energy to build some massive pyramids. The laser-like energy, powered with quartz crystals, was used to position the huge sandstone blocks so accurately that a folded piece of paper could not be passed between pieces of stone weighing tons.

The bases of the pyramids were made from granite, which contains 20–40 per cent quartz crystal. By building the pyramids on granite the priests knew that the immense pressure of the sandstone blocks above would activate the crystal energy found naturally in the granite, thus creating a gigantic generator. This powerful energy field could then be utilised by the priests for healing and religious ceremonies. The pyramids were sheathed in sandstone and chalcedony to form a resonator and each pyramid was given a capstone of pure quartz crystal. Sadly, the quartz crystal capstones have been vandalised and stolen through time and are now no longer in evidence.

The ancient Egyptians believed that all quartz crystal was sacred. They made their cups and mugs out of quartz, and whenever they drank from one of these cups, they received an intake of life-giving energy. They also created the most exquisite jewellery and ornaments out of amethyst, lapis lazuli and quartz crystal, some of which may be seen in the British Museum in London.

Lapis lazuli was a particular favourite of the Pharaohs, who used to wear the stone around their heads. They believed that by wearing lapis lazuli in this fashion they would receive a great deal of power and energy which would help them to rule authoritatively over their subjects.

Akhnaton

Akhnaton — the so-called heretic Pharaoh of the eighteenth dynasty — may have been a reincarnation of an Atlantean high priest. He had great knowledge and wisdom. There was, in Akhnaton, an immense power of devotion which he directed to the one God, whose beauty overwhelmed him and whom he saw as the power behind the sun.

Mona Rolfe, the great Irish seer, in her book *Initiation By The Nile* provides us with a marvellous insight into the character and person that was Akhnaton:

> To Akhnaton the sun was the most glorious sight and he wanted all men to share his knowledge. He believed that if he could build the perfect city and a temple that would be supreme in its glory, then men would see it as an expression of truth and recognise the value and worth of the teaching.
>
> Akhnaton was a genius, a great soul who drew his inspiration direct from God. To him the sun was the most glorious sight of all. But he did not worship the sun, he worshipped the one invisible God — whose symbol the sun was. He was hated by the priesthood when he sought to effect changes in the form of worship in the temples. He realised the necessity for the multiplicity of gods, that each one had his place. But he knew that there was one God above them all — and that he could communicate direct with God in the silence of his own heart. He told the priests that all men could communicate direct with God — and this they did not like; they did not wish to have the power taken out of their own hands, for they had accumulated great wealth through the power they held.
>
> Many souls who are incarnate today are incarnate from bodies which they held in the time of Akhnaton. Through study, meditation and concentration, at this moment the incidents in which we were concerned can be built through our ancient memory, and in remembering we may not only help to bring to light knowledge

which will be of importance to the archaeologists and others, but also will link the path of our own soul with the paths of others who trod the self-same way with us during that particular dynasty.

You believe that the tomb of Akhnaton has been discovered and all that was in it has been revealed. This is not so. His tomb lies as yet untouched, undisturbed, three storeys below ground level of the Temple of Thebes. Many discoveries will be made of the first layer of that ancient temple, much will be found of the second layer dealing with matters concerning the great Atlantean temple; then, at the third layer, shall we find this vast and glorious temple within which the body of Akhnaton is held in reverence and light.

Although the tomb is very deep below the level of the sea there is no sign of damp, or the ravages of water, of mildew, or the ravages of creatures.

The tomb itself is made of transparent stone, stone which was used in the great Temple of Atlantis and in Persia for the healing beds; in some lights it looks of one colour only; in others it looks of many colours; the rays of the Place of Light pass through it and enfold it, beating their power into the earth, drawing from the sand a great light and using it for the preparation of yet further rays, which will eventually guide those who hold the key to the tomb. None other may approach it.

The coffins, or sarcophagi, lie side by side with one another; in the one the magnificent figure of Akhnaton and in the other lies the figure of Hareth, his wife; and that you may know she is Hareth when you hear of her finding, you will remember that about the brow she bears a golden circlet, wide, soft, which though restraining the tresses it leaves no impress upon the delicate brow itself. In the centre of that golden band is a mighty ruby, shining as no ruby you have every seen shone before. The hands are delicate, cared for and beautiful.

Outside the tomb, at either end, will be discovered two small chambers, so small that a man would have difficulty in standing upright therein — but these are merely boxes of records. In the box placed at the head of the young King and Hareth will be found a manuscript in ancient script giving the clue to the last books of Genesis; in the other will be found a script in Aramaic, but written long before anyone speaking Aramaic, or writing Aramaic upon the tablets approached the Court of Egypt.

These scripts will need special readers, only one or two, who have been trained under the guidance of Oneferu, ninth master initiate from Atlantis, who will be able to read them, only these will be able to place them in their proper position in the Book of Genesis and in that last book which should follow the writing of the Revelation of St.John — the book which closes that book of Scriptures which you know as your Bible.

The pathway to the tomb is in darkness; men must traverse the temple and many passages are sown with white stones — the white stone representing the Light of the Spirit, stones just large enough for a man to hold in the palm of his hand. When the right man treads the passage the stones lift, the light shines and he walks forward to the tomb itself, where he will be called upon to worship, for God in His Holiness is the guide and strength of mankind, the director of the life of man and the mighty works of God.

Several esoteric sources refer to the fact that 'records' detailing Atlantean technology will one day be discovered in a secret chamber in the hidden tomb of Akhnaton. Also mentioned on more than one occasion is the idea that Akhnaton's tomb — and the hidden chambers — will only be discovered when the right person or persons are present.

The New World

The American Red Indians were also great believers in the healing power of crystals and gemstones. Personal stones would be given to a baby boy at birth and throughout his adulthood, until death, the Red Indian would carry these crystals and gemstones around with him in a specially designed pouch attached to his waist. Red Indians have always possessed tremendous insight and knowledge, often intuitive, about the natural laws of mother earth. They speak about crystals with a perception that comes from deep in their hearts and minds.

The Red Indian Legend of the Crystal Kingdom

The Bear tribe, chief among the animals, called a meeting of all the animals. They decided that something just had to be done about the destructive tribe of Mankind. The Bears suggested that they shoot back when the humans shot at them, but the bow and arrow required too great a sacrifice, for one bear would have to give up his life so that his sinew could be used for the bowstring. The bear's claws were too long for shooting a bow anyway, and would become entangled on the string.

The Deer tribe offered another method of dealing with the problem. One of its members said, 'We will bring disease into the world. Each of us will be responsible for a different illness. When humans live out of balance with Nature, when they forget to give thanks for their food, they will get sick.' And, in fact, the Deer did invoke rheumatism and arthritis; each animal then decided to invoke a different disease.

The Plant tribe was more sympathetic and felt that this was too harsh a punishment, so the plants volunteered their help. They said that for every disease a human suffered, a plant would be present to cure it. That way, if humans used their intelligence, they would be able to cure their ailments and regain their balance.

All of Nature agreed to this strategy. One plant, in particular, spoke out. This was Tobacco, the chief of the plants. He said, 'I will be the sacred herb; I will not cure any specific disease, but I will help people return to the sacred way of life, provided I am smoked or offered with prayers and ceremony. But if I am misused and merely smoked for pleasure, I will cause cancer, the worst disease of all.'

The close friends of the Plant tribe, the Rock tribe and the Mineral tribe, agreed to help. Each mineral would have a spiritual power, a subtle vibration that could be used to regain perfect health. The Ruby, worn as an amulet, would heal the heart; the Emerald would heal the liver and eyes, and so on.

The chief of the mineral tribe, Quartz Crystal, was clear, like the light of creation itself. Quartz put his arms around his brother Tobacco and said, 'I will be the sacred mineral: I will heal the mind and help human beings see the origin of disease. I will help to bring wisdom and clarity in dreams. And I will record their spiritual history, including our meeting today, so that in the future, if humans gaze into me, they may see their origin and the way of harmony.' And so it is today.

This legend is part of the heritage of the Cherokee tribe; yet it has been told, and retold, time and time again, by every Red Indian tribe.

Crystals and Gemstones in The Bible

Crystals and gemstones have a number of very important biblical associations. The children of Israel (Exodus 28:15–21) made a breastplate of judgement for Aaron which included settings of four rows of precious stones; the first row was a sardius, a topaz and a carbuncle; the second row was an emerald, a sapphire and a diamond; the third row was a jacinth, an agate and an amethyst; the fourth row was a beryl, an onyx and a jasper. All these stones, in the four rows, were set in gold.

In the Garden of Eden itself (Ezekiel 28:13) were to be found many precious stones including sardius, topaz, diamond, beryl, onyx, jasper, sapphire, emerald and carbuncle.

In the very last chapter of the Bible — the Revelation of St John the Divine — St John talks of a new heaven and a new earth, and a new Jerusalem coming down from God, made ready like a bride prepared for her husband. John is shown a great vision of this new Jerusalem. It shines with the glory of God; it has the radiance of some priceless jewel, like a jasper, clear as crystal. It has a great high wall, with twelve gates, at which are twelve angels; and on the gates are inscribed the names of the twelve tribes of Israel. There are three gates to the east, three to the north, three to the south and three to the west. The city wall has twelve foundation stones and on them are the names of the twelve Apostles.

The walls are built of jasper, while the city itself is of pure gold, bright as clear glass. The foundations of the city wall are adorned with jewels of every kind, the first of the foundation stones being jasper, the second, lapis lazuli, the third, chalcedony, the fourth, emerald, the fifth, sardonyx, the sixth, carnelian, the seventh, chrysolite, the eighth, beryl, the ninth, topaz, the tenth, chrysoprase, the eleventh, turquoise and the twelfth, amethyst. The twelve gates are twelve pearls, each gate being made from a single pearl. The streets of the city are made of pure gold, like translucent glass.

The Amethyst

Amethysts were always very popular in the old civilisations around the Mediterranean Sea. Beautiful beads, exquisitely carved from amethyst, were used as early as the first dynasty in Egypt, some 5000 years ago.

There is a legend surrounding the origins of the name 'amethyst' which explains its connection with modesty and how it came to be a purplish colour. According to the legend, Bacchus, the god of wine, had been slighted and vowed to take his revenge on the first person to come along. So he ordered his tigers to eat whomsoever happened to walk by.

Fate dictated that a maiden named Amethyst was on her way to worship at the Temple of Diana, a goddess associated with modesty, when the tigers attacked her. The girl appealed to Diana for help and in a second the goddess turned her devotee into a statue of clear crystal. Seeing all this, Bacchus regretted his anger and he poured a cup of wine over the crystal statue, thus creating a rich purple-hued stone.

2

Choosing, Cleansing and Dedicating Crystals

All crystals and gemstones, like human beings, 'vibrate' on their own individual frequency. We have all had the experience of meeting a perfect stranger for the very first time and either liking that person immediately or feeling an antipathy towards them, without in any way being able to explain our emotions. Falling in love is a similar experience: the coming together of two minds, two spirits and two physical bodies, both 'vibrating' on the same wonderful frequency! Crystals and gems should be chosen in exactly the same way. It is very important that the stones we use should 'vibrate' on a frequency as close as possible to our own.

Individual methods of choosing crystals and gems vary from person to person but normally include the following:

1 Close your eyes and quietly meditate for a few moments. Then open your eyes very quickly and pick up the first stone to which your eye is naturally drawn.
2 Run your hand (either left or right) over all the stones. You will soon discover that one stone will 'stick' to your hand as if it is 'tacky'. This is your stone.
3 You will instinctively know which stone you should choose. You might feel as if the stone is jumping up and down and shouting, 'Me! Me! Choose Me!'
4 You might sense a strong white light radiating from the stone and attracting you like a magnet.
5 If you are a competent dowser then you should be able to select

the most appropriate stone by using your own individual dowsing techniques.

6 Sometimes you feel as if your stone actually chooses you! This is quite true. My most powerful and important crystals have all arrived on my doorstep (so to speak) for a particular purpose and have usually either been absolutely free or cost me very little money.

Should you wish to choose a crystal or gemstone for a friend who perhaps lives some distance away from you, follow exactly the same principles as if you were choosing a personal stone for yourself but this time visualise, as strongly as possible, an image of your friend in your mind's eye. With a little practice you will discover that it is very easy to select just the right stone for someone who is absent.

There are very many people who, for one reason or another, are unable to obtain crystals or gemstones. In such cases it may be possible to work on the name vibration alone or the vibrations emanating from a letter. From all the feedback I receive from people for whom I have performed this service, it would appear that in most instances this method works very well.

Research is also being carried out to see whether it is possible to determine through the use of computer technology which crystal or gemstone vibrates on a particular individual's frequency. Using special equipment it is possible to analyse the vibrations of each person and show this information by means of a graph on the computer screen. Experiments to analyse the vibrations of every crystal and gemstone using such techniques are continuing and eventually it will be possible to compare one set of vibrations with another, using a specially written computer programme which will enable anybody to find the right crystal or gemstone for them to work with.

Cleansing your Crystal

Having chosen your crystal (whichever method you may have used) it is now essential that you cleanse it. Crystals and gemstones easily attract all sorts of vibrations, negative as well as positive. They are always open to receive impressions from everyone and everything around them. Your stone may well have travelled many thousands of miles before reaching you, and will probably have acquired many negative energies and vibrations in its long journey to find you.

Before starting to use your stone for any purpose whatsoever it is very important that you first remove any of these unwanted negative vibrations and energies. You must ensure that only the most natural — and pure — energies remain.

The cleansing method used is a matter of personal choice, or the actual time available, but I strongly recommend that you use one of the following cleansing methods, which I have found to be very successful:

1   Hold your stone in either your left or right hand and say, 'I will and command that this stone be self-cleansing'. As you say these words (mentally or verbally) you should visualise the negative energies falling away out of your stone and only the natural, and pure, energies remaining.

2   Water is a universal cleanser: hold your stone under cold flowing water from the tap (cold or luke-warm water only) and, again, visualise the negative energies and vibrations being washed away and only the natural, pure, energies remaining. Never attempt to dry your stone with a cloth after cleansing in water. Always allow it to dry naturally — preferably in the rays of the sun. The sun, of course, is a very powerful energiser and should be used whenever possible. If there is little or no sun readily available, then you should allow your stone to dry as naturally as possible in the warmth of your house.

3   Immerse your stone in salt water for several hours. Dry as above.

4   Bury the stone under the earth in your garden. The very strong magnetic energy field in the earth will cleanse your stone of its negativity very effectively.

5   Place your stone on a large quartz crystal cluster for a few hours. The strong energies present in the cluster will ensure that any negative energies in your stone are easily neutralised.

Dedicating your Crystal

As all crystals respond instantly to the 'intent of will' of the person using them there is always a distinct possibility that, in certain circumstances, crystal energy may be abused or misdirected.

(Indeed, it is thought by those who ascribe to the theory of the downfall of Atlantis that its eventual destruction was caused through the gross misuse and abuse of the sacred crystal energy and power by some of the priests in Atlantis.)

It is said that those priests who were corrupt became extremely power-conscious and began to use crystals for their own egocentric ends. They endeavoured to create immoral and unethical deviations from the normal patterned structure of crystal energy. They experimented by 'inter-breeding' incompatible sources of energy and power which resulted in the creation of new vibrational frequencies which they could have under their personal control. These new vibrations were then implanted within the cells of other living creatures, which led to terrible physical and mental deformities. The children of many of these deformed creatures feature in many of the myths that have been perpetuated from time immemorial. Monsters, some half-man, half-beast, demons and giants appear to have been let loose for many thousands of years. Finally, they were all destroyed before they could be allowed to upset the vibrational balances of the energies of mother earth.

In the wrong hands, crystal energy may be used for evil or negative purposes. Therefore, it is very important that we use our crystals and gemstones for only the very highest of purposes. It is up to each one of us, in our own way, to protect our own crystals and gemstones against all negativity, misuse and abuse.

Crystals always attract inquisitive minds and hands (children and adults alike!) and many of these transmit negative energy vibrations. To protect your stones from all potentially harmful energies and vibrations simply hold the stone in your hand and say the following few words, 'I will and command that this stone be only used for the highest benefit of myself and the people with whom I work'.

Your stone has now been cleansed and dedicated and is ready for 'programming'.

3

Programming your Crystal

All crystals and gemstones will respond to your intent of will; whether in word or thought. By simply wishing — or visualising — the crystal energy to be used in a particular way, it will be! Crystals are usually 'programmed' for meditation, healing, absent healing and manifesting.

Meditation

Every day of the week, every minute of the day, throughout the world, countless thousands of people practise their own form of meditation, each person finding solace in their own particular way.

By holding a quartz crystal or amethyst in your hand whilst practising whatever type of meditation is appropriate to your own particular needs, you will enhance and enrich the spiritual depths of your meditative experience. The amethyst is known for being able to relieve mental and physical stress and tension. It is the stone of quietude; the stone of peace and tranquility.

The quartz crystal or amethyst enables you to undertake a new and wondrous journey within your soul. Pathways, hitherto uncharted, will open up before you. A new dimension of self-expression will rise to the surface and expand your inner consciousness and awareness.

Each member of your meditation group should have his or her own piece of quartz crystal or amethyst to hold throughout the meditation session. As time passes, perhaps very slowly at first, each person will gradually become aware that his or her breathing has become deeper and more rhythmical and that he or she has entered a completely new world of inner peace and harmony.

All meditation rooms would benefit from having large quartz crystals placed in all four corners of the room with their single-terminated ends (the six-sided facet at one end of the quartz crystal) directed towards the centre of the room. These crystals should be placed either on the floor or affixed to the ceiling. Each crystal should be programmed to project gentle, loving, relaxing energy towards all those in the meditation group. The crystals will generate a field of positive energy at all times. In addition, a large display amethyst or quartz crystal may be placed in the middle of the group. This large stone should then be 'programmed' to release beautiful cosmic energies into every part of the room. One member of the meditation group must be nominated to look after the group's crystal or amethyst, and to make sure that it is properly cleansed, dedicated and programmed.

When holding your crystal or amethyst and meditating with music you will discover that some amazing effects are often produced. On some occasions you might even be able to 'see' the music in terms of colour and shape. Even just listening to a piece of music whilst holding your stone — and not consciously trying to meditate — you will find the depth of experience greatly enriched by the presence of your crystal or amethyst. It is as though the mood and thoughts of the composer become deeply embedded within the very heart of the crystal and if you 'listen' to the crystal afterwards with your inner ear, in a meditative state, you will often be able to appreciate the esoteric meaning of the music itself.

Practising Meditation

Now we are ready to try our own crystal meditation. I would suggest that you hold either a personal quartz crystal or a piece of amethyst in whichever hand you feel to be most appropriate.

First of all, lie or sit in a very comfortable position. Relax and breathe slowly. Say a prayer of protection, perhaps the 'Great Invocation', or your own impromptu prayer.

Now hold your crystal between your hands and locate the opening to the crystal. Do this by slowly and sensitively rubbing your thumbs and fingers across the faces of the crystal, moving from one face to another. The objective is to find a spot where your thumb or finger sticks like glue onto the crystal. This is your opening into the crystal and into the crystal energies. Close your eyes, if you have not already done so. Breathe slowly and deeply. Relax all your muscles starting with your feet and gradually working your way up through the rest of your body till you arrive at the head.

First exhale and then inhale and exhale again, allowing yourself to relax and ridding yourself of all the internal stress within your body. Allow your body to sink deeper and deeper into the floor. Let go; hold nothing back. Allow your head, and now your neck, to relax, and continue letting go of all the tension.

Relax your throat and then your shoulders, letting the burdens fall off them onto the floor. Let your arms and your fingers relax, feel the tension being released.

Now relax your chest, back, spine and abdomen; breathe slowly and deeply. Inhale, exhale, allow the tension to fall off your body and onto the floor. You don't need it any more. Now your waist, buttocks, pelvis, thighs, knees, calves and feet: relax each of them in turn. Let *all* the tension go. Again, breathe slowly and deeply, inhaling, exhaling.

Now bring your awareness to your crystal between your hands. Turn your attention to the entry point into the crystal and merge with the crystal and with your breath. Together exhale, inhale and focus on your entry point and then exhale again, merging and merging more fully into the crystal. Release your expectations, your thoughts and personality — and surrender to your own inner being. Let all the inner tension slowly rise to the surface and let it all drop off your body and onto the floor.

Let us now fully merge with the crystal. Let us inhale, exhale, inhale, focusing on the entry point. Exhale. Feel the crystal energies engulfing you, enveloping you, surrounding you. Allow your senses to become very acute: your sense of touch and taste, smell, hearing and sight, as you begin touching the wall of the crystal. Notice the temperature, taste the crystal energies, listening, listening for any sounds, voices, noises. Expand your vision. Look around to see what it feels like to be within a crystal, to be within these exquisite energies.

Allow yourself to breathe deeply, relax, heal. Become aware of your every breath and how relaxed your whole body has now become. There is nothing to do; there is only to be and feel these healing energies. Breathe the love into you, take it in. Allow the healing to go deeper and deeper within, into your core, the very essence of your being, your soul and your spark of divine life.

When you have received all the healing, released all the tension within your physical and mental bodies, and received all the healing energy that you need, gently, slowly, your consciousness is pulled to the wall of the crystal. You recognise that you are very relaxed and stress-free, and that as you return to your every-day existence you will be a changed person because of this profound experience of deep love, this new understanding that is now yours, that has gone so deep within your soul and the very essence of your own divinity.

Notice how you are feeling and recognise that at any time you can return to the crystal energies. Now, however, it is time to release yourself from the crystal. Leave as you entered; exhale, inhale, focus on releasing from the crystal; exhale, letting go, relaxing, breathing evenly and less deeply. Withdraw yourself from the crystal, slowly, once again inhaling deeply, and focus on receding further from the crystal. Exhale, withdrawing your energies. Then place the crystal by your side. Say a prayer of thanks for all that you have received. And now slowly begin drawing your arms over your head in a lazy stretch. Begin moving your fingers and toes. Now you are back in your own room.

There are many other forms of crystal meditation that you might try. For example, turn out all the lights in your room and sit in a comfortable chair in front of a table with a lighted white candle on it. Place a quartz crystal upright in front of you with the lighted candle behind it. Make sure the crystal is at eye-level. Look at the flame of the candle through your crystal and gradually become aware of your breathing, in, out, in, out, slowly relaxing. Continue to gaze into the flame, aware of your body breathing slowly and rhythmically, becoming more and more relaxed.

If you find that random ideas and thoughts keep passing through your mind, allow them to come and go gently; let them be free to roam. Keep gazing into the flame and become still within yourself. Let your breath slow down and your whole body metabolism become calm and peaceful.

Try to do this meditation at least once a day for 40 minutes. You will soon find that your whole being becomes calm, peaceful, and relaxed!

Healing

Once you have chosen your quartz crystal, cleansed and dedicated it, you are ready to commence using it for healing. It is very important to note, however, that your quartz crystal should be used *either* for healing or for meditation, not both. The vibrations and energies used in healing and meditation are very different, and to use the same quartz crystal for both purposes would result in the dissipation of the crystal's energies.

Quartz crystals are, in reality, only tools. By themselves they can only be described as passive, but when they are activated by the human mind they can become very powerful indeed. Each one of us possesses an inherent healing energy. In most people, of course, this ability lies totally dormant, but when we are able to channel our own healing energy through a quartz crystal the healing power is amplified and the energy thus created — our own in conjunction with that of the crystal — may be used for many positive purposes.

Even though you may not wish to become a qualified crystal healing therapist there are still plenty of opportunities for you to use your quartz crystal to treat your family and friends.

When my youngest child, Cameron, was only a few months old I returned home from giving a crystal healing workshop one day to discover that he was very poorly. My wife had taken him to our local doctor who had told her that if he did not improve within the next couple of days he would have to go into hospital.

When Cameron was ready for bed that evening I cradled him in my arms and placed an electro-crystal therapy 'wand' (see p. 64) on his stomach. I also took my personal healing quartz crystal and directed its healing energy to completely envelop his body. I gave him healing for 30 minutes only, at the end of which he was fast asleep.

The next morning he was almost completely cured, and there was no need for him to go back to the doctor or to go into hospital.

Healing Sessions

At the beginning of your healing session you should hold your quartz crystal in whichever hand feels right to you; and calmly attune yourself to the inner energies of your crystal. You will probably experience the pulsation of the crystal energies throbbing in your hand.

Direct the single-terminated end of your quartz crystal towards your patient and gently move the crystal around the perimeter of the whole body in a clockwise direction. Do this several times. This will help to strengthen the bio-magnetic energy field of the patient's body.

The single-terminated end of the quartz crystal should then be directed towards that part of the patient's body which you believe to be most in need of healing. Visualise, as strongly as possible, a lovely blue-white light emanating from the apex of your crystal and being directed, like a laser beam, to that part of the patient's body needing healing. The blue-white light becomes stronger and brighter, and the energy between the crystal and your patient slowly intensifies.

The healing session may last any length of time but intuitively you will become aware when the time is right to conclude the session. To end the healing treatment you should visualise the blue-white light gently flowing back into your quartz crystal. Once more you should direct the energies of your crystal around your patient in a clockwise manner. Then allow your patient to relax for a few minutes. Whenever practical it is best for your patient not to drive a car for some time after the crystal healing session as patients often become so very relaxed that it can take some time to re-orientate themselves!

From my own personal experience I have found that it is not always necessary to know in advance what is wrong with your patient. I believe that all dis-ease arises purely as a result of an imbalance of our normal bodily vibrations. Therefore, whatever health condition we may suffer from, however serious or mild, the treatment remains much the same (although no guarantee of a cure or improvement can be given). All that is necessary is that the imperfect or imbalanced vibrations are re-harmonised, re-energised and re-balanced. This may seem like an oversimplification but experience has shown me that all too often we can overcomplicate the situation!

Once you have programmed your quartz crystal for the benefit of your patient the healing connection between the crystal and the patient will remain in force until you re-cleanse your crystal, and when a healing link has been created, the healing energies of the crystal are 'activated', 24 hours a day, 7 days a week, and 52 weeks a year, until the programme is erased by you when cleansing your crystal.

You may also use your quartz crystal for self-healing purposes. All you have to do is direct the single-terminated end of your crystal towards the appropriate part of your body and, as before, visualise the lovely blue-white light radiating from the apex of your crystal like a laser beam, into your own body.

Crystal healing can certainly be a very powerful way of re-balancing, re-energising and re-harmonising every part of you or your patient's physical and mental body.

Absent (Distant) Healing

Quartz crystals are often used very successfully in all forms of absent — or distant — healing. Whether you are 3 miles, 300 miles, or 3,000 miles away from your patient, crystal healing can be most effective.

It is only necessary to know the name of the person who wishes to receive absent healing, which, using the power of crystals, works on the name vibration. Visualise the energy which is pulsating within your absent healing crystal being projected towards your patient, wherever he or she may live. If you possess a photograph of the patient — or if you have met the person and know what they look like — hold your crystal in your hand and visualise, as strongly as possible, the crystal energy totally surrounding the patient. You may also place the absent healing quartz crystal on the photograph which helps to amplify the energy being projected from the crystal towards the patient.

It is best to use absent healing quartz crystals for no other purpose. In my own healing sanctuary I have a master absent healing quartz crystal which I use for all my absent healing work. Whenever requests are received for absent healing I inscribe the name and relevant details in my absent healing book and then place my master absent healing quartz crystal on top of the book and programme it so that *every* name entered in the book will receive healing from the crystal energies, each according to his or her needs.

I also ask everybody to try and link up with my master crystal at 10 pm every evening, but I tell my patients that healing rays and energies will be directed towards them on a continuous basis.

Manifesting

Very simply, manifesting is a method of programming your crystal to help your subconscious mind to create something in your life that you *need*. Before proceeding, however, it is very important that you know what you wish to achieve. Decide, in as precise detail as possible, what you wish to obtain. Need, not want, should be your main criterion. For example, you might say that you want to win a huge amount of money. But that is most definitely a want, not a need!

There was once a man who desperately desired a Rolls-Royce. He could think of nothing else. So he used his crystal to 'manifest' one. He visualised a Rolls-Royce for days on end, until, at last, his dearest wish was granted. A Rolls-Royce went out of control and crashed through the window of his front room! A classic instance of not making it clear exactly what he wanted. And it was a want, not a need — so be warned.

Now, make yourself comfortable in your easy chair in order to begin to manifest your inner needs: hold your quartz crystal in front of you, with both hands. Stare at it and visualise yourself entering the crystal through a door cut into it. Once through this door you will find yourself in a long narrow hall, at the end of this hall is a green door with the words 'Manifesting Room' written upon it.

Open the door of the manifesting room, step inside and look around. The walls are solid gold; the floor is green; and the ceiling is studded with millions of precious gemstones, sparkling with all the colours of the rainbow. The room is filled with a warm, rich feeling of prosperity.

Bring into your mind a complete image of whatever it is you wish to manifest. Visualise as much detail as possible; concentrate as hard as you can and imagine that you actually possess whatever it is you are manifesting. You are extremely happy and relaxed, secure in the knowledge that your need has been met.

Take your time; 5, 10, or even 15 minutes, it doesn't matter. Then, when you have finished, slowly walk back out of the manifesting room, closing the door firmly behind you, walk back along the hall and step outside the crystal. Take a deep breath, relax your body and when you feel really comfortable, open your eyes.

Do your manifesting twice a day (morning and evening) until your need has been fulfilled.

4

Healing Properties

Throughout the ages, mankind has been aware that certain gemstones possess therapeutic healing properties. In all four corners of the world, crystals and gemstones have been used in many different ways to heal the sick in mind, body and spirit.

The following information has been compiled from many different sources and may be used as a reliable guide when deciding which stone would be most appropriate in any particular case.

Agate A stone for general healing purposes; helps improve the ego and self-esteem, improves vitality and develops powers of eloquence.

Alexandrite Helps the nervous system, spleen, pancreas and testicles. Can be used to amplify colour therapy.

Amazonite Regulates and improves thinking abilities.

Amber Used for rheumatism, intestinal disorders, earache, bladder trouble and asthma. Can absorb negative energy and helps the body heal itself.

Amethyst Used in meditation and for general healing purposes. Helps people suffering from stress and tension. Affords protection against blood diseases, neuralgia, fits, grief and insomnia.

Apatite Strengthens muscular tissue and aids in co-ordinating basic motor responses. Helps people suffering from stuttering and hypertension.

Aquamarine Helps nerve, gland, throat, liver and stomach troubles. Relieves toothache. Improves sight.

Aventurine Good for skin diseases. Improves vitality.

Azurite Gives relief from arthritis and joint disabilities. Reduces hip joint pain. Helpful in meditation.

Beryl Improves intellect, strengthens will-power. Helps heart problems, liver trouble, mouth, stomach and throat infections.

Bloodstone Strengthens the will to do good. Improves liver, kidneys and spleen.

Blue Quartz Helps improve heart, lungs, throat and thymus. Good for people suffering from emotional traumas. Aids the release of inner emotional tension from deep within the body.

Calcite Helps kidneys, spleen and pancreas. Helps remove toxins from the body. Alleviates mental fear.

Carnelian Strengthens the voice. Helps people suffering from rheumatism, arthritis, depression and neuralgia. Aids sense of touch. Used for infertility and impotence. Alleviates blood poisoning, fever, infection, nosebleeds, sores, spasms and wounds.

Chalcedony Improves bone marrow, spleen, red corpuscles and heart tissue. Stimulates optimism and enhances spiritual and artistic creativity.

Chrysocolla Helps relieve nervous tension.

Chrysolite Strengthens the appendix. Alleviates general toxaemia and viral conditions.

Chrysoprase Improves prostate gland, the testicles, Fallopian tubes and ovaries. Increases fertility in both men and women.

Citrine Helps improve blood circulation. Gives the wearer control of the emotions.

Coral Good for anaemia, bladder conditions, colic and whooping cough.

Diamond A master healer! An extremely powerful stone in the removing of blockages and all emotional negativity.

Emerald Improves intellect and memory. Helps cure insomnia. Improves eloquence.

Fluorite Strengthens bone tissue, especially teeth enamel. Relieves dental disease, pneumonia, viral inflammation.

Galena Strengthens lungs, thyroid and nervous system. Protects against depression and skin diseases. Promotes self-confidence, pride and success. Improves imagination. Helps people suffering from depression.

Garnet Protects against depression and skin diseases. Promotes self-confidence, pride and success. Improves imagination. Helps people suffering from depression.

Haematite Improves all blood disorders.

Herkimer Diamond Releases stress and tension throughout body.

Ivory Protects physical body from injury.

Jacinth Promotes spiritual sight and understanding. Used in childbirth, helps insomnia.

Jade Mainly used for kidney complaints and bladder trouble.

Jade (green) Comforts stomach disorders, eases eyestrain and aids function of the liver.

Jade (red) Combats female disorders, aids ovarian and uterine functions.

Jasper Improves sense of smell. Helps with kidney, liver and epilepsy problems, biliousness, bladder trouble, and stomach trouble.

Jet Prevents deep depression.

Kunzite Alleviates anaemia. Improves general tissue rejuvenation.

Lapis Lazuli Helps heart and spleen. Protects against epilepsy and strokes. Helps people suffering from depression.

Lazulite Improves pineal glands and liver.

Lazurite Stimulates visions. Can amplify thought-form. Also used for tissue rejuvenation.

Magnetite Stimulates endocrine system. Improves blood circulation. Helps in meditation.

Malachite Helps asthma, toothache and irregular periods. Improves eyesight. Aids rheumatism.

Moonstone Gives inspiration. Encourages personal attachments. Helps soothe and balance emotions.

Obsidian Snowflake Helps sharpen internal and external vision. Balances stomach and improves general muscle tissue.

Onyx Aids concentration. Helps hearing problems. Good for heart trouble and ulcers.

Opal Helps lung conditions. Increases assimilation of protein.

Pearl Promotes antibodies and fights infection.

Peridot Aids digestion. Can cleanse and heal hurt feelings. Improves bruised eyes and helps mend damaged relationships.

Petrified Wood Restores physical energy. Helps hip and back problems. Aids past-life recall.

Pyrite Aids digestive system of abdomen and upper intestinal tract. Eases anxiety, depression, frustration and false hopes. Strengthens astral body.

Quartz Used for general healing purposes. Assists wearer to think intuitively.

Rhodochrosite Prevents mental breakdowns, balances physical and emotional traumas. Improves kidney, pancreas and spleen.

Rhodonite Restores physical energy (especially following trauma or shock). Strengthens inner ear and improves sense of hearing.

Rhyolite Rejuvenates physical beauty. Helps to increase self-expression, and to speak with greater clarity.

Rock Crystal Used to relieve diarrhoea, dizziness, haemorrhage, kidney trouble, spasms, and vertigo. Helps to ease pain anywhere in body.

Rose Quartz Has a calming effect on emotions. Helps people suffering from emotional trauma. The love stone.

Ruby Strengthens intuitive faculty and aids initiative. Improves fever, pain and spasms.

Rutile Quartz Helps people suffering from bronchitis.

Sapphire The stone of friendship and love. Gives wearer devotion, faith, imagination and peace of mind. Helps bleeding, insomnia and nervousness.

Sardonyx Stimulates self-control and protection.

Smoky Quartz Used for good luck talisman. Helps to protect soldiers on active service. Improves abdomen, kidneys, pancreas and sexual organs. Increases fertility in both men and women.

Sodalite Helps logical and rational thought, and intellect.

Spinel Attracts help. Makes wearer strong in character.

Sugilite (from South Africa) Restores balance in pineal, pituitary and left and right brain hemispheres. Improves autism, dyslexia, epilepsy, physical co-ordination problems, visual problems. Helps spiritual awareness.

Tigers Eye Helps people gain insight into their own faults. Helps people think more clearly. Good for asthma.

Topaz Helps improve blood circulation. Improves varicose veins. Improves sense of taste. Good for insomnia, liver trouble and nervousness.

Tourmaline Attracts inspiration, good will and friendship. Bestows self-confidence on wearer. Useful for meditation. Protects wearer against misfortune and anaemia. Prevents lymphatic diseases.

Turquoise Protects wearer against harmful vibrations. Used in meditation. Aids intuition. Can strengthen entire anatomy and helps improve all diseases.

Zircon Helps liver complaints; an all-round healer.

Although, quite obviously, no guarantee of any cure or improvement can ever be given, there are many occasions when the above-mentioned stones have considerably helped to improve many different diseases and health conditions.

From personal experience I have found that the most effective way to use any gemstone for healing purposes is to have it as close to the skin as possible. The vast majority of people prefer to wear their chosen gemstone around their neck on a silver- or gold-plated chain. In addition to the healing energies of the gemstone being able to penetrate the body more easily, the gemstone pendant is a beautiful piece of jewellery — and is always aesthetically pleasing to the eye!

Gemstones may, if desired, be held in the hand whilst you are watching television during the evening, or reading a favourite book or magazine. Others prefer to place their gemstones under their pillow at night whilst they are asleep; thus allowing the energies of the stone to gently operate throughout the course of the night.

The healing and relaxing power of crystals and gemstones has even reached boardroom level. In recent exhibitions, for example, I have sold some fairly large amethyst clusters to managing directors, sales directors, etc., who have acquired their amethyst clusters to place on their office desks — or in their boardroom.

Certain stones can help you to develop your spiritual abilities and gifts. Use an amethyst for developing your intuitive awareness; a lapis lazuli for acquiring wisdom and truth; and a moonstone for obtaining humanitarian love and sensitivity. Use your gemstones wisely in the pursuit of all your ambitions and needs. However, be aware that your gemstones can never become miracle workers. They need your loving care and attention, and your mental attunement with their unique properties and energies, before they are truly able to help you.

5

Birthstones

There are twelve signs of the Zodiac; Aries, Taurus, Gemini, Cancer, Leo, Virgo, Libra, Scorpio, Sagittarius, Capricorn, Aquarius and Pisces.

I am constantly asked during the course of my workshops and seminars to recommend an appropriate stone for a particular birth sign. In my experience the only accurate way to ascertain which birth stone is applicable to a particular person is for that person to visit a properly qualified astrologer and for a detailed chart to be constructed, based on the person's place of birth, date of birth and exact time of birth. Any other method is too vague and generalised.

A few years ago I scrutinised as many books as I could lay my hands on which contained information relating to the astrological use of gemstones. From all the information available I compiled my own comprehensive chart — birth sign by birth sign — including all the recommended birth stones which each book suggested would be appropriate for each sign of the Zodiac. When my task was completed I discovered that every birth sign had at least *nine* gemstones which, according to all the books, would be suitable for people born under that particular sign of the Zodiac.

Nevertheless I find the following chart useful as a guide (and a guide only!) when I am asked to recommend a particular stone for a person's birth sign.

Aries jasper, ruby
Taurus rose quartz, lapis lazuli, carnelian, sapphire
Gemini citrine, rock crystal, tiger's-eye, agate, rutile
Cancer olivine, emerald, moonstone

Leo quartz crystal, diamond, agate
Virgo carnelian, agate, jasper, sapphire
Libra emerald, aventurine, jade, sapphire
Scorpio garnet, bloodstone, ruby, jasper, beryl
Sagittarius topaz, jacinth, obsidian, snowflake
Capricorn smoky quartz, ruby, onxy, jet
Aquarius turquoise, malachite, aquamarine, moonstone
Pisces amethyst, opal, moonstone

6

Pyramids and Crystals

Pyramids, and the aura of mystery surrounding them, have always fascinated the scholar, the archaeologist and lay-person alike. The ancient Egyptians were not the only people to build pyramids. In South and Central America, for example, a number of large pyramids have been discovered. I also believe that in Atlantis there were several crystal pyramids. When the time came for Atlantis to be destroyed, those priests who were allowed to leave, and who were transported to the four corners of the world, took their knowledge of pyramids with them.

Most of the pyramids, of course, are to be found in Egypt. According to the historians and archaeologists the Pyramid Age of Egypt began in the Third Dynasty (2686 B C) and ended in the Sixth Dynasty (2181 B C). During this Pyramid Age around 80 pyramids were constructed. Many of these pyramids are no longer immediately recognisable as such as they have been reduced to nothing more than sand and rubble, but the Egyptian archaeologists, through years of painstaking work, have managed to identify where most of the pyramids would once have stood.

Throughout the years considerable controversy has arisen with regard to precisely why the pyramids were built in the first place. What purpose did they serve? Egyptologists themselves claim that the pyramids were erected simply as tombs; whilst other archaeologists, excavating pyramids in South America, have advanced the theory that they were used as temples.

Recently, some pyramidologists have stated that they believe that the pyramids are possibly resonators, or storehouses, of energy. Certainly, this is an explanation that is finding great support nowadays.

The largest pyramid of all — and one that is still standing today, having stood the test of time and the weather — is the Great Pyramid of Giza, also known as the Pyramid of Cheops, who was a Pharaoh who reigned in the Fourth Dynasty (around 2450 BC). The pyramid is 146 metres (481 feet) high and 230 metres (756 feet) square at its base, and is a mathematical phenomenon.

The Great Pyramid was the seventh wonder of the ancient world. It consists of some 2,500,000 limestone blocks, each weighing between 2 tons and 70 tons. These blocks, which require 2 tons of pressure on a diamond bit merely to drill a hole into, are cut with a tolerance of 1/1000 inch, and fitted like a jigsaw puzzle.

The pyramid is built on the exact mathematical ratio of pi: 3.14159, the ratio of a circle's circumference to its diameter. It has been calculated by mathematicians that if, during construction, 10 of these stones were placed on each other with precision every day, some 500 tons a day on average, the pyramid would have taken some 250,000 days, or 664 years, to complete. And one may also like to note that, officially anyway, the true value of pi was not discovered until 600 years ago!

The Great Pyramid's four triangular faces incline at an angle of approximately 51 degrees, 52 minutes to the ground. The entire pyramid was originally built in line with true north.

Arguments and controversy have always surrounded the Great Pyramid of Giza, and probably always will. For although most Egyptologists, scientists, and scholars do agree that the Great Pyramid was built by Cheops somewhere between 2686 and 2181 BC (many favouring the year 2450 BC), there is no definite evidence that the pyramid was actually built then; and most psychics, sensitives and seers believe that it was built many thousands of years before 2450 BC and was used for purposes other than a tomb.

Manly P. Hall, in *The Secret Teachings of All Ages*, alleges that the pyramid was constructed by people arriving from Atlantis after it was destroyed. He propounds the theory that the Atlanteans established centres of education and learning, built in the form of pyramidal temples, in which they hid their esoteric secrets, 'written' in symbolic language, to be discovered and understood only by those who were worthy of acquiring and using this sacred knowledge.

According to Hall, there is a great mystical knowledge hidden in the inner depths of the pyramid. The square base means that the pyramid is solidly founded on nature and its immutable laws; the angles represent silence, profundity, intelligence and truth. The south side of the pyramid signifies cold, the north side represents heat, the west side symbolises darkness, and the east side, light. The triangular sides typify three-fold spiritual power. Hall goes on to say that he is certain that there is a hitherto unknown room or chamber within the pyramid which will one day be rediscovered.

It is worth recounting the strange experience of Dr Paul Brunton which he describes in his book *A Search in Secret Egypt*. After going through the Egyptian bureaucratic hierarchy, he succeeded in obtaining permission to spend a night inside the king's chamber of the Great Pyramid.

Dr Brunton says that on entering the king's chamber he found a marble slab next to the large coffer, which, incidentally, is exactly aligned on the north-south axis. Dr Brunton had had some training in the Egyptian religion and was also quite knowledgeable about some of the more recent discoveries in parapsychology. He had therefore prepared himself by fasting for three full days before his night in the pyramid. This put him in a receptive frame of mind to experience whatever phenomenon existed there.

Sitting with his back to the great coffer, Dr Brunton decided to turn off his flashlight. An unknown negative presence could be felt, and he experienced a strong urge to leave the chamber. Grotesque and deformed entities flitted in and out; it took every ounce of courage he possessed to fight off his fear. The combination of darkness and the negative presences convinced him that he would never spend another night in the Great Pyramid.

Then, as suddenly as the negative atmosphere had come, it dissipated. He felt, at first, a friendly air come alive in the chamber. Next, he could see in front of him two figures who looked like high priests and, suddenly, inside his head he heard one of the priests asking why he had come and if the world of mortals wasn't enough for him. Brunton answered, 'No, that cannot be'.

The priest replied, 'The way of dream will draw thee far far from the fold of reason. Some have gone upon it — and come back mad.

Turn now, whilst there is yet time and follow the path appointed for mortal feet.'

Brunton insisted that he must stay. The priest who had spoken to him turned and disappeared. The other priest told him to lie upon the coffer, just as had the initiates of old. As he did so, a force came over him, and in a few seconds he was hovering outside his body. He was in another dimension of less stress and strain. He could see a silver cord connecting his new body with the one lying on the coffer. He became aware of a feeling of freedom.

Later, Brunton found himself with the second priest, who told him that he must return with a message: 'Know, my son, that in this ancient Temple lies the lost record of the early races of man and of the Convenant which they made with the Creator through the first of His great prophets. Know, too, that chosen men were brought here of old to be shown this Covenant that they might return to their fellows and keep the great secret alive. Take back with thee the warning that when men forsake their Creator and look on their fellows with hate, as with the princes of Atlantis in whose time this pyramid was built, they are destroyed by the weight of their own iniquity, even as the people of Atlantis were destroyed'.

As the priest finished speaking Brunton suddenly found himself back in his own body. He felt it to be cumbersome compared to the one he had just inhabited. He got up, put on his jacket and checked his watch. It was exactly 12 midnight, the hour that is customarily associated with strange events.

Biocosmic Energy

A few years ago, a Frenchman by the name of Monsieur Bovis paid a visit to the Great Pyramid of Giza. There were some rubbish containers in the king's chamber in which Bovis could see various dead cats and other small animals which had apparently wandered into the pyramid and died of starvation. There was something very strange about these corpses: there was no smell or decay at all! His curiosity aroused, Bovis examined the animals very carefully and discovered that they were dehydrated and mummified, despite the humidity in the king's chamber.

Bovis pondered this apparent conundrum and wondered whether the pyramidal shape itself could have been responsible for this natural process of embalming. So he made a wooden scale model of the Great Pyramid of Cheops with a base 1 metre (3 feet) long, and oriented it to true north as was the Great Pyramid. Inside his model, a third of the way up, he placed a dead cat which had only recently died. After a few days, it became mummified. Bovis then experimented by placing other organic materials in the model, particularly matter that usually decayed very quickly, such as calf's brains, and when these failed to putrify, he reached the conclusion that there must be something about the shape of the pyramid which prevents decay and causes dehydration.

A Czechoslovakian radio engineer by the name of Karel Drbal obtained, by chance, a copy of Bovis's reports and decided to make some further experiments himself with models of pyramids. His conclusions were: 'there is a definite relationship between the shape of the space inside the pyramid, and the physical, chemical and biological processes going on inside that space.'

Drbal also considered that the pyramidal shape might also be responsible for an accumulation of electromagnetic waves or cosmic rays, or of some unknown energy. Placing a used razor blade within a 15-cm (6-inch) high model of Cheops' Pyramid, facing true north, Drbal found that the edges of the blade automatically recovered their sharpness after use, and that he could shave with one razor blade as many as 200 times! He believed that the environment inside the pyramid somehow made the crystals in the blade return to their original form. Drbal was issued Czech patent number 91304, after a long fight, for the Cheops Pyramid Razor Blade Sharpeners.

An Italian milk company has started putting their milk in pyramid-shaped cartons. They have discovered that such milk keeps indefinitely without refrigeration. A French company even patented a pyramidal container for yoghurt a few years ago.

In March 1963, biologists at the University of Oklahoma confirmed that the skin cells of the Egyptian Princess Mene were capable of living — although Princess Mene has been dead for several thousand years!

In my healing sanctuary I have now erected a 2.5-metre (8-foot) high pyramid, in which I do all my healing sessions. The results have been very good indeed. Merely stepping inside the pyramid has an immediate calming effect upon the nervous system and leads to a slowing down of the rate of body metabolism. The pyramid appears to have the ability to amplify the energies present within the structure, which leads to wonderful healing power being created.

Pyramids are also very effective for all forms of meditational purposes. Many people claim they experience feelings ranging from calmness to extreme euphoria during their meditation sessions. I myself always feel as if I am being lifted out of my body and being levitated through space and time. Most people who have experimented with large pyramids report that they start by experiencing a total relaxation of the body, then a kind of shutting out of unnecessary external stimuli and irrelevant thoughts and finally they achieve an altered state of consciousness which allows them to concentrate on deeper inner levels.

Pyramids may help you to reduce the level of stress and tension in your body. You may attain a heightened charge of psychic energy, increased memory recall, views of past incarnations, dreams, visions of indescribably beautiful colours, forms, shapes, symbols, or music 'from the spheres'. Some people experience precognition, interplanetary travel, telepathic communications, answers to prayers and overall revitalisation of their entire being.

From my own experience I have discovered that through working with my crystals within the pyramidal structure I am able to substantially increase the level of healing vibrations, with excellent results.

The 2.5-metre (8-foot) pyramid in my own healing sanctuary is constructed out of thickish copper tubing, which always acts as a conductor of energy. I place four large quartz crystal clusters at the four corners of the pyramid, which help to balance the energy field created. Most of my treatments take place on my massage couch, specially designed so that its height is approximately one third of the height of the pyramid's apex. The couch is also aligned on a true north/south axis. You could even try placing a plant under a smallish pyramid — and watch it grow. Research has shown that seeds germinate faster and plants grow quicker when placed within the energies of a pyramid.

7

Crystal Dowsing

Although I prefer to use a quartz crystal pendulum for any dowsing which I wish to do, it is not strictly necessary to use a crystal. Any gemstone pendant, for example, will do just as well. Whatever you use, whether it be a crystal pendulum or gemstone pendant, it is essential that you harmonise and attune your higher self with your dowsing instrument.

To achieve the best results I find that I need a chain-length of around 15–23cm (6–9 inches). Before commencing to dowse with my crystal pendulum I first establish which direction it will swing for 'yes' and which for 'no'.

I suspend the pendulum over my left hand, palm upwards, and mentally request the pendulum to swing in the direction of 'yes'. In my case this is usually in a clockwise circle. I then ask it to change direction and show me which way is 'no'. For me, this is normally side to side.

It is very important that you go through this same routine *before* you commence every dowsing session as it is possible, from time to time, that the pendulum will reverse directions. In most instances, however, it will remain the same.

Now you are ready to begin. Only ask the pendulum questions that can be answered 'yes' or 'no'. Try to work in a quiet room away from electrical equipment such as televisions and computers, as electromagnetic 'disturbances' or energy fields may influence your results. I always try to spend a few minutes in quiet meditation before beginning a dowsing session as it is easier to obtain true results if one's mind is uncluttered by material thoughts and ideas! Your inner emotional state of mind may also affect your results so try and remain as detached as possible from the work you are doing.

I find that everything becomes possible through using my crystal pendulum. Answers to difficult questions can easily be obtained. All it needs is plenty of practice. After a while you will discover that on occasions your pendulum will start to swing violently in one direction or another when you ask it your question. And if you go on to ask it your next question it will change its direction just as violently.

Your crystal pendulum may be used to advise you which crystal or gemstone to use in your healing sessions. Or which stone to purchase when you are faced with a bewildering choice. At my crystal healing workshops and seminars more and more people are now choosing their crystals and gemstones by this dowsing method. And it appears to work very successfully for them.

On rare occasions you will find that your pendulum refuses to move in any direction. Usually this occurs when the question you have asked is one to which it is not appropriate for you to know the answer — after all, there are some things that one simply has to work out for oneself! You must also try not to use your pendulum in too trivial a fashion. Asking the pendulum whether you should go to your local supermarket today, or wait until tomorrow, for example, is a total waste of the pendulum's energies and yours, too! Use your pendulum wisely and it will become one of your most trusted friends.

If you are an aromatherapist you will find your pendulum very helpful in selecting the best combination of natural oils for your patient. If you are a nutritionist then the pendulum can help you give the best possible advice to your patient and it can also assist you in discovering any allergies from which the patient may be suffering. The list of possibilities is almost endless. Some dowsers specialise in finding missing people (particularly children) through the careful use of maps. Others are experienced in finding underground water supplies. And some are employed to recommend suitable areas to drill for oil.

One of my students has devised his own dowsing rod, which has two small crystals fixed at either end. With your patient standing up straight you place one hand on one side of the body and the dowsing rod opposite your hand on the other side of the patient's body. You then move your hand and the dowsing rod slowly down the patient's body. Wherever an imbalance exists or where healing is necessary then the dowsing rod will move slowly towards the patient's body. In my experience, once you have dowsed a few times, this method becomes almost infallible and acts as a very good check on other methods of diagnosis.

On occasions I also use a more conventional set of dowsing rods. Two wire coat-hangers will do if you can't acquire the real thing!

It is very interesting to be able to detect the energy field that has been created, for example, around my massage couch after I have been working with crystals for a few minutes on my patient. The energy field is dowsed before the treatment commences. Usually this simply shows a passive field extending maybe 7.5–10 cm (3–4 inches) on each side of the couch. However, a further reading, a few minutes later, when the patient is lying on the couch and surrounded by crystals will often show an energy field extending several feet around the couch. Sometimes I cannot measure this field accurately because it extends beyond my healing room.

Kirlian Photography

Kirlian photography was first invented by a Russian husband and wife team, Semyon and Valentina Kirlian. It is a system of high-frequency photography that can be used very effectively to detect psychological disorders and physical ailments before the symptoms manifest themselves visibly.

For many centuries, seers and psychics have claimed to be able to see people's 'auras'. An aura is described as a luminescent quality which completely surrounds the human body, and may be seen in different colours. It is these colours that the seer or psychic is able to interpret by relating to the health condition of the body.

After a great deal of research the Kirlians appeared to have discovered a method of actually photographing an aura. When Kirlian photography was used to photograph a leaf which had just been parted from its parent tree, for example, beautiful radiant colours were observed in the photograph. However, as time passed, and the life-force in the leaf began to fade, subsequent photographs showed the colours becoming dimmer and dimmer until eventually they disappeared altogether when the leaf was finally dead. Obviously, if this technique could be used on leaves, it could be tried on human beings. And that was exactly what the Kirlians went on to do.

Early research results encouraged some scientists in the belief that Kirlian aura photography could be very useful in the future as an accurate diagnostic tool. However, Professor Arthur Ellison of the City University in London, in an objective assessment, has pointed out that it would be difficult to use Kirlian photography as a diagnostic technique because there are too many variables involved, any of which may affect the final analysis.

8

Chakras and Crystals

The word '*chakra*' comes from the Sanskrit word meaning 'wheel'. If we were able to see the *chakra* (as many seers and psychics do) we would see a wheel of energy continuously revolving or rotating at specific sites on the human body.

There are seven major *chakra*s:

First *chakra* base of the spine
Second *chakra* spleen, or sexual centre
Third *chakra* solar plexus
Fourth *chakra* heart
Fifth *chakra* throat
Sixth *chakra* third eye, or brow
Seventh *chakra* crown, or head

The *chakra*s play a very important part in our work with crystals. Any imbalance in the *chakra* may have profound effects on either our physical or spiritual bodies. We can use quartz crystals to rebalance our *chakra* centres and once the *chakras* are balanced then the body will gradually return to normal.

The first, or base *chakra* is located at the bottom of the spine. This is where the *Kundalini* is situated. This *chakra* is associated with the colour red. It is a very important centre as it has so much effect upon the rest of the body. I find that I am able to release a great deal of the physical stress and tension of the nervous system by working on the base *chakra* with my crystals.

The second, or spleen *chakra* is located in an area bounded by the spleen and sexual centre. This *chakra* is associated with the colour

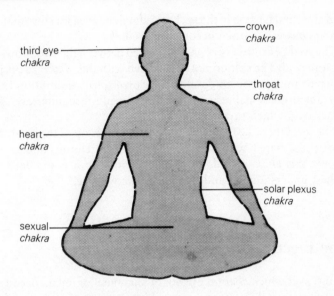

Figure 1   View of frontal *chakras*

orange. Usually, people suffering from sexual blockages need heal-ing here.

The third, or solar plexus *chakra* is located in the solar plexus just below the navel. This *chakra* is associated with the colour yellow. There are often large amounts of physical energy and power within the third *chakra* or emanating from it, and it is also the psychic storehouse of mystical energy, used by materialisation mediums for producing ectoplasm and other psychic manifestations.

The fourth, or heart *chakra* is located in an area in the centre of the chest, between the two nipples. The colours associated with this *chakra* are green and pink. I use the heart *chakra* to help people suffering from emotional traumas and problems in their rela-tionships. A piece of rose quartz or blue quartz helps to release their inner emotional tension or torment.

The fifth, or throat *chakra* is located in an area that corresponds to the centre of the throat. The colours associated with this *chakra* are blue and turquoise. When people suffer from headaches (perhaps migraine) and tension in the neck and shoulder muscles I find that the throat *chakra* has often become blocked.

The sixth, or third eye *chakra* is located between the two brows on the forehead. The colour most associated with this *chakra* is purple. When helping people to develop their own spiritual intuition I find that amethyst, sodalite, lapis lazuli or luvulite (sugilite) are ideal stones with which to work.

The seventh, or head *chakra* is located on the top of the head. The colour associated with this *chakra* is white. During any crystal healing this *chakra* needs to be open. Through it is obtained the highest understanding and the highest knowledge.

The Electro-Crystal Scanning Meter

To discover which *chakras* are out of alignment or imbalanced I use an electro-crystal scanning meter, which in my opinion is one of the most exciting current developments in the field of crystal healing. When using the meter I am able to scan the whole body from head to toe and the meter accurately records all variations in the patient's normal energy vibrational pattern.

Having established where all the *chakric* imbalances lie I am now ready to begin using my crystals with the specific intention of rebalancing, reharmonising and re-energising the patient's body.

The electro-crystal scanning meter will often show a patient as having one or more *chakras* out of alignment or imbalanced. The twelve-crystal configuration (see Chapter 13) will usually correct these imbalances automatically within 20–25 minutes. Once the treatment has finished I rescan the patient with my electro-crystal scanning meter and 95 per cent of the people I treat show a very great improvement with all the body energy systems totally back to normal!

Another excellent technique that I use for balancing the *chakras* involves the patient lying on his or her back with crystals placed upon the body in the following fashion: two crystals should be placed on the third eye *chakra*, point downwards. Two crystals should be placed on the palms, point upwards; two crystals on the breast area, point upwards; and two crystals on the top of the thighs, point upwards.

If the patient then lies quietly on his or her back for about 15 minutes the *chakras* will quickly re-align themselves. Again, this can be easily verified with the electro-crystal scanning meter.

9

Electro-Crystal Therapy

The technique of electro-crystal therapy has been researched and pioneered in the UK by Harry Oldfield, originally a school science teacher who developed an interest in Kirlian photography from a project for his school science club. He managed to build his first Kirlian machine from a set of instructions and eventually became so intrigued by the possibilities created that he left his teaching position and devoted himself to full-time research and treatment.

Harry Oldfield is now one of the leading researchers and exponents in the field of Kirlian aura photography in the United Kingdom. He has developed his own Kirlian camera. Using just two fingers of each hand he is able to interpret the health conditions of the patient. Harry can usually confirm that the patient has or does not have cancer, or even that he or she is a 'cancerous' person and might suffer from cancer some time in the future.

With Glen Rein, an American biochemist then at Queen Charlotte's Hospital in London, Harry Oldfield investigated a series of tissue specimens from women with breast cancer. He found that the light intensity emitted in the Kirlian camera from cancerous tissue samples was considerably greater than that coming from healthy tissue. Accordingly, he extended the scope of his work to include Dr Peter Kandela, a general practitioner associated with one of London's leading hospitals. A small series of Kirlian photographs of the hands of cancer patients showed similar increases in their discharge pattern compared with normal women.

Harry then arranged a clinical trial involving 100 women to see how accurately cancer could be diagnosed using such Kirlian techniques. Unfortunately, the trials had to be cancelled as his proposal never received approval from the various hospital committees that have to agree to such investigations. For them it was far too speculative.

Harry faced the problem that many natural health practitioners who are engaged in research seem to face: the 'catch-22' situation that orthodox medicine will only listen to those in the complementary medicine field when they are able to produce some positive proof to substantiate their claims, but such 'proof' can only be obtained from medically monitored clinical trials carried out in a medical environment, under medical supervision and involving medically qualified personnel.

Harry has admitted that the lack of clinical trials is always going to be his main problem in getting his electro-crystal therapy work accepted by the medical profession, but he is not downhearted. His School of Electro-Crystal Therapy is producing many qualified electro-crystal therapists and Harry's research work marches on with gratifying rapidity.

The electro-crystal therapy unit can work off either two 9-volt batteries or the mains. However, I normally only use batteries as I feel that this is the safest method, and avoids the possibility of a sudden upsurge in the electrical supply whilst I am treating a patient.

The unit consists of a rectangular box with two dials, one showing the letters, A,B,C, and D, the other the numbers 0–10. These two dials control the frequencies of electromagnetic energy that is used in the treatment. Attached to the unit is a sealed glass tube or wand. This tube contains very small gems and/or crystals, in a solution of salt water. The stones are stimulated with various different electromagnetic pulses.

Pulsed high-frequency electro-magnetic energy can, of course, be effective in its own right, but then combined with crystals and gemstones the healing effect increases beyond all recognition. I have treated a wide range of health conditions from migraines to multiple sclerosis, from cancer to glandular fever, and every person treated has reported *some* improvement in their condition. I always stress, however, that there is never any guarantee of a 'cure' taking place. I am satisfied merely if my patients feel that I have managed to help them in some way.

As mentioned previously, in order to obtain full medical backing and support we need to monitor our patients for many years to see the long-term effects of our electro-crystal therapy treatment. For example, do the symptoms return, perhaps in five years' time? Or is it a permanent cure? Natural remission and positive affirmations by both therapist and patient also have to be taken into account. There are many factors which need to be considered before making too many claims. But the fact that, at present, we have obtained some excellent results is very encouraging. (Some members of Harry's School of Electro-Crystal Therapy have also been treating some of our animal friends including cats, dogs and horses, with much success. In cases like these the power of auto-suggestion can, I believe, be ruled out!)

When treating a patient with the electro-crystal therapy technique the glass tube or wand is placed against the area of the body where the pain occurs, or where treatment is deemed necessary, or against the appropriate *chakra*. The wand is usually fixed in place with a strap and the unit is switched on after the dials have been set to the correct frequency for the treatment.

Although the thick glass tube itself is a superb insulator, a secondary field is set up by the electro-magnetic induction. Harry believes that this occurs when the electrical field passing through the stones picks up the healing vibrations of each stone, so that in effect the electrical field is acting as an amplifier and carrier wave. This theory cannot be proved at present but it does seem to be very effective.

One way of monitoring the effect is by removing the stones from the wand altogether. If this is done and the wand is again placed against the relevant area of the body, very few, if any, healing pulsations are felt and no change takes place in the patient's health condition. This appears to indicate very forcefully that the addition of the stones and crystals is essential if healing is to take place.

An advantage of electro-crystal therapy (which applies to crystal healing as a whole) is that there are no harmful side-effects. On occasions patients do comment that they are feeling very tired or even very relaxed at the end of a treatment session but this is probably a purely natural reaction of the body, not previously in balance with itself, and needing a recuperation period before the full healing effects of the therapy can be felt.

One positive side effect which does occur quite frequently in many patients is that, in addition to their health condition improving, the patient begins to notice an increase in vitality and energy, in both physical and mental bodies. There are also patients who have come to me for the treatment of one health condition and who have come back for further treatment saying that not only had that condition improved but that other health problems, which they had not mentioned to me, had also improved.

One very elderly lady came to me for treatment of paralysis. She had suffered a stroke some months previously and as a result the left side of her body was totally paralysed. When she returned for her next treatment session she reported that not only was she beginning to feel some sensations returning to her left arm but that she was now able to breathe properly for the first time in ten years! Apparently, her nose had been blocked up continuously in that ten-year period but she had not thought to mention it to me when we first met.

All the crystals and gemstones in the wand attached to the electro-crystal therapy unit are programmed to *heal*, and their healing energies result in balance and harmony being restored to all the body's fields with which they are in contact. This will occur in any of three ways: the healing energies will *tranquilise*, i.e., reduce, those energies which are in excess; they will *stimulate*, i.e., increase, those energies which are deficient; and they will *balance*, i.e., bring into proper proportion, those energies which are out of balance with each other.

You should think of your body as encased in electrical chain-mail (the radiation force-field); illness in the body distorts the chain-mail. You must first treat the symptoms on the actual site (the distortion in the chain-mail), by placing your wand on the site of the problem and setting your dials to balance, stimulate or tranquilise according to need. This treatment usually reduces, or may completely eradicate, the symptom. But it is only the symptom that disappears; not the actual cause of the problem. Your next placement of the wand should be to treat the current flows of the meridians and particularly the huge flow (the river mouth; of the *chakra* associated with the site of the symptom. Every part of the body relates to one or more *chakras*. The meridians are the streams and the *chakras* are the river mouths.

When you treat the *chakra* point you must firstly ensure that the river mouth is open to the flow of energy and that this energy can enter or leave as a tide in or out of a river mouth. Then the energy will disperse itself through the streams (the meridians associated with the *chakra*) to nourish the body.

The head *chakra* and the third eye *chakra* are connected to the mental processes, the brain and the eyes. They stand apart from the other *chakras* and meridians, and are also the sites of the symptoms. For treatments involving the throat *chakra* the wand is placed across the throat or the back of the neck. This *chakra* affects people suffering from cervical lesions (conditions of the neck and top of the spine), and problems with ears, nose, mouth, throat, migraine and high blood pressure. It also treats the lungs, through an associated meridian, and the large intestine, which is connected by meridians to the lungs.

For the heart *chakra* the wand is placed directly over the heart. This *chakra* affects people suffering from tachycardia (irregular pulse beat), problems in the lungs, angina, tension, aortic regurgitation, bronchitis, emphysema and pleurisy. Through its meridian linkage the heart *chakra* can also treat the small intestine. The thymus, the gland which activates the auto-immune system, is located just above the heart *chakra* and treatment here can help people suffering from colds, flu, hay fever and allergy effects on the eyes.

For the spleen *chakra* (located below and to the left of the heart *chakra*) the wand is placed over the spleen area on the body. This is the *chakra* to treat cancer, duodenal ulcers, pancreas and stomach problems, indigestion and hiatus hernia. For the solar plexus *chakra* (located at the top of the stomach) the wand is placed directly over the solar plexus. This is the *chakra* relating to problems with the adrenal glands (the body's alarm system) and anxiety. It is also a *chakra* which can lose energy. Treatment should be undertaken on this *chakra* where the patient suffers from loss of energy, collapse and debility.

The base *chakra* is located at the bottom of the spine, and for this *chakra* the wand will be retained in position if it is pushed horizontally into the top of the trousers or tights. This is a very important *chakra* point, relating to the bladder through the meridian linkage, the kidneys, spine, back pains (requiring daily treatment), rheumatism, sexual organs, legs and feet. It also affects pre-menstrual tension.

Harry stresses that although in his experience every patient enjoys a positive benefit from receiving treatment from his electro-crystal therapy machine and wand one should always respect the skill of the doctor and conventional allopathic medicine. The patient should never be discouraged from consulting the doctor or hospital, as they too have an invaluable role to play in the well-being of the patient.

10

Crystal Sound Therapy

As an extension of electro-crystal therapy, Harry Oldfield has also designed a machine for crystal sound therapy, which also incorporates an electro-crystal therapy unit. The principle upon which his system operates uses highly tuned electro-magnetic waves to excite individual crystals to such a very high level that they begin to emit audible sound waves, each quartz crystal having its own individual note.

How is crystal sound therapy used?

We have already learnt from previous chapters how to programme our own crystals. If we programme a quartz crystal and place the crystal upon the surface of the crystal sound therapy machine, we can then pulsate an electro-magnetic energy through the crystal, liberating the programme into the atmosphere. This enables the therapist to be able to treat a number of patients, suffering from more or less the same health conditions, at the same time. Even deaf people and people with hearing difficulties have received benefit. Crystal sound therapy has obvious advantages, in time considerations alone, if one is able to treat, say, a dozen people suffering from cancer all at the one time.

Everyone reacts in different ways to the crystal sound vibrations. I am always very interested to observe the reactions of my students when they are first exposed to the vibrations at my workshops or seminars. Some people feel a tightening across the brow, others experience a tingling sensation in their fingers and toes. Some people tell me that they can feel their solar plexus vibrating — or perhaps one of their other *chakras*.

When demonstrating the crystal sound technique in front of my students I always pre-programme the quartz crystal with the intention that every person will receive crystal healing energy according to their particular needs. The results can often be astonishing. Without having told the group what it is I have done, I am usually told by many of those present that they can feel the energy from the crystal entering their body at a point where they know already that they need treatment. It seems as if the crystals possess an intelligence greater than we think and that they know almost automatically where to send their 'love' and energy to the patient.

Crystal sound therapy also works very well in meditation groups. By pre-programming a quartz crystal to assist each member of the group to relax and enter a new and wonderful state of inner consciousness, a completely new experience often occurs. Environments and atmospheres may also respond, almost immediately, to the positive vibrations emitted through the crystal sound therapy machine. 'Heavy' atmospheres may become lighter, fresher and purer. Some people find that crystal sound therapy is as effective, if not more so, than traditional ionisers.

11

Crystal Wands

The crystal wand is one of the most powerful forms of 'light tool' presently known to mankind. The wand itself consists of a hollow copper tube of about 30 cm (1 foot) in length. The copper tube should be around 2 cm (¾ inch) in diameter. A quartz crystal of about 7.5 cm (3 inches) in length and around 2 cm (¾ inch) wide, clear and with reasonably unchipped facets, is affixed to one end of the copper tube. At the other end of the tube is affixed either a copper cap or another quartz crystal. Either single- or double-terminated quartz crystals may be used. The whole copper tube is insulated by a leather strip wound completely around the wand.

The best way to discover exactly how a crystal wand functions — and its tremendous potential as an energiser — is to make one for yourself. By constructing your own crystal wand, your own vibrations will merge with that of your wand.

To make your own crystal wand, first take your hollow copper tube and, with a hacksaw, cut two lengthwise strips at one end of the tube, about 7.5 (3 inches) deep. Then, with a pair of pliers, bend the sides outwards so as to allow room for your quartz crystal. Glue the sides of the crystal before gently sliding it into its place in the copper tube. You must now bend the sides back into place and ensure that at least 2.5 cm (1 inch) of your crystal protrudes at the end. At the other end of the tube, either glue the copper cap into position or affix another quartz crystal.

Finally, take your leather strip (any colour will do) which should be about 1 metre (3 feet) in length, and place small amounts of glue at intervals on one side. Then tightly wrap the leather, in spiral fashion, around the copper tubing. Your crystal wand is now ready.

When your wand is lying by itself it is in 'passive' mode but as soon as you pick it up it becomes operational or in 'active' mode. Crystal wands are very simple to operate. All you need to do is pick up your wand, focus the energy by thinking of a blue-white light of energy radiating from the apex of the quartz crystal, and you have created your own powerful ray of energy and power. You must use your new tool wisely.

At the first workshop after I had constructed my first crystal wand, I was holding it in my right hand whilst I was talking and, without thinking, I must have directed the wand at the third eye *chakra* of one the students present. With a yell the student nearly toppled back on his chair. Apparently he had experienced a tremendous burst of force from my wand which had almost hurled him back in his seat. Be very careful, therefore, where you point the wand when you are holding it.

For ordinary healing purposes I use my wand in much the same way as an ordinary quartz crystal. I take my wand in my right hand and move the wand around the patient's body, in a clockwise fashion, for a few moments. I then focus the energies of the wand through the apex of the quartz crystal and directly into the body of the person whom I am treating. I find that about 15 minutes is sufficient at any one time. After directing the healing energy into the patient I finish by moving the wand around the perimeter of the patient's body for a few moments. Using this technique the patient's body becomes surrounded by a field of crystalline energy which penetrates every fibre of the patient's inner and outer being, and, in most cases, a healing effect occurs.

As soon as I pick up my wand the whole wand begins to vibrate and pulsate. My hands begin to tingle and I feel alive with crystal energy and power. I channel my own healing energies into the wand which further amplifies them, and by the time the healing rays leave the crystal at the end of the wand a truly powerful source of energy has been created.

I am often asked at my workshops and seminars why it is necessary to insulate the wand with leather. Insulation is essential for your own protection as I have found out from personal experience: when working with the wand for any length of time, a great many subatomic particles accumulate within the copper tube and on occasions, if you touch the actual copper, you may receive an electrical-type shock. This has happened to me on more than one occasion in my experimental work.

The results you are able to obtain by using a crystal wand depend upon your own ability to attune yourself at a high enough level with all the vibrational energies at your disposal. Like everything else in life, the more you practise the more you achieve! As your energies become stronger, your wand will grow more potent, too. Crystal wands never break down, need no external power source, and can be used 24 hours a day, seven days a week. The possibilities are unlimited.

Crystal wands may be used for purposes other than for healing. For example, one evening I had to give a talk at a town some 50 miles from where I live. I was late; I had been delayed and I knew that time was short. I came off the motorway and found myself engulfed in traffic being held up by a continuous system of red traffic lights.

By a strange coincidence my crystal wand was lying on the passenger seat next to me. Without really thinking what it was I was doing I idly picked the wand up with my left hand and focused it on the next red traffic light; it turned to green! And so it went on, every red traffic light, virtually instantaneously, turned to green when my wand was directed at it. I thus managed to arrive at my meeting dead on time. Strange, but true.

Why not construct your own crystal wand, and discover for yourself all it can do?

12

Crystal Massage

Crystal massage can be a really beautiful and uplifting experience, working on a deep esoteric level. Not only does the physical body enjoy total relaxation but all the inner emotional stresses are brought skilfully to the surface of the mind — and dissipated.

For many years now I have been practising as a qualified massage therapist and also as a qualified tutor of massage. My treatments have involved several different kinds of massage ranging from Swedish massage to intuitive massage. When I began using crystals in my healing work it seemed perfectly natural that I should also use crystals as an extension of my massage treatment. There are many and varied ways of using crystals to enrich and enhance the massage experience.

The delight in using a single-terminated quartz crystal with unchipped facets, directly upon the patient's body, should never be underestimated! Using a single-terminated crystal, crystal massage may be divided up into two categories: where a basic knowledge of the techniques of massage are essential, and where it is not necessary for one to have any knowledge of massage at all.

In the first category I prepare a patient in exactly the same fashion as if he or she were going to have an ordinary massage. I use my massage couch and the patient begins the session by lying on his or her stomach so that I may start by working on the back area. I always use massage oils and the massage session takes roughly the same format as always. When I have finished the normal massage treatment, I pick up my personal quartz crystal and, very gently, massage the entire body by stroking the single-terminated end of the crystal against their skin. I usually commence with the feet, move upwards slowly to the head and then back down the body again.

The secret of a successful crystal massage lies in being able to control the crystal so that it almost glides over the surface of the patient's skin. Before you begin using your crystal it is important that you first programme it for the benefit of your patient. I always mentally attune myself with the crystal by asking that the crystal energies penetrate the skin of the patient and balance, re-energise and re-harmonise every part of their body.

In the second category of crystal massage it is not necessary for you to have any basic knowledge of massage at all. Instead of using oils and hand massage techniques you move straight on to using the quartz crystal. The effects can often be absolutely delightful. As you progress and become more experienced in crystal massage you will be able to massage body, mind and spirit at the same time, and once you have mastered ordinary crystal massage techniques you can move on to practising more advanced crystal massage.

For the more advanced techniques I dispense with my massage couch and use the floor itself. It is not quite as comfortable as using the couch but there is a great deal more room in which to work and the floor affords you greater opportunities for using new forms of crystal configurations.

The patient lies on his or her back in the middle of the floor. I then place between 12 and 30 large quartz crystals around the body with all the single-terminated ends of the crystals pointing inwards (see Figure 2). I try to place all the crystals at equidistant points around the body in a circular fashion, allowing me enough room to work on the patient whilst I am also inside the circle. The energy field thus created is extremely strong and the energies from each crystal combine to provide a unified magnetic energy field, which penetrates every fibre of the patient's body and mind.

Working on a patient who is lying within the energy field is a joyful experience as both patient and therapist are able to share in the wonderful relaxing vibrations that continue to emanate from the crystals whilst the treatment is progressing. A deep therapeutic crystal massage will often lead to the inner release of emotional traumas and tensions — of which the patient was probably totally unaware!

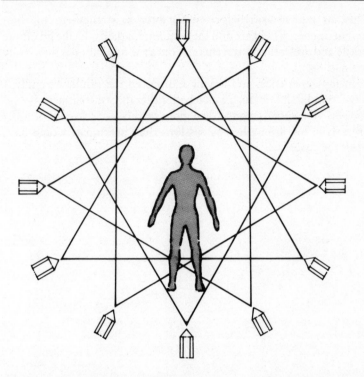

Figure 2   Crystal massage configuration

At present not many massage therapists are aware of the value of using crystals in their massage sessions. The future, however, should see a gradual awakening of interest and a desire for knowledge that will see more and more people being introduced to the exciting world of crystal massage.

Besides massage I also practise aromatherapy (the art of using and blending essential oils in massage). I often use quartz crystals to increase the potency of the essential oil. Having once chosen and blended the most suitable combination of oils for my patient I take up my personal quartz crystal and move the crystal around the perimeter of the bottle containing the oil in a clockwise direction.

This, as I have said before in Chapter 3, strengthens the bio-magnetic energy field around the container. I then take the lid off the bottle and direct the crystal energies onto the oil. The oil is then ready for use.

In my experience, and having monitored the results carefully, I have found that I obtain a much better therapeutic treatment — and the patient responds a great deal more readily — as a result of using crystals in my aromatherapy sessions than previously would have been the case.

13

Crystal Configurations

There are several kinds of crystal configurations which I wish to share with you. I am indebted to Frank Alper, of the Arizona Metaphysical Society in America, for introducing me to this very powerful and potent form of crystal healing. In his trilogy of books *Exploring Atlantis* he expounds many different healing methods — including the configurations — which may once have been practised by the priests in the days of Atlantis. Since first meeting Frank in London several years ago I have been using crystal configurations in practically all my healing treatments.

Randall and Vicki Baer, in their comprehensive book entitled *The Crystal Connection*, include a great many wonderful advanced crystal configurations and crystal gridworks. In most instances they are very complex and beyond the understanding of the majority of therapists. I hope to maintain simplicity as a keynote to all the configurations which I am going to share with you.

In crystal healing we seldom try to diagnose a patient's health condition in normal layman's or medical terminology. All disease or illness is regarded as an imbalance of the normal level of vibrations. In using crystals, our main purpose is always to redress the imbalances of the patient's physical and mental bodies. No cures can ever be guaranteed, but improvements can, and do, regularly occur. Even though the medical profession may still regard crystal healing as 'fringe' medicine, it is very encouraging to note that more and more doctors are now contacting us with a request for further information about crystal healing. A few are even using crystals in their own allopathic medicine.

The Twelve-Crystal Configuration

Probably the most common crystal configuration, and one which I use very frequently, is the twelve-crystal configuration; it is the one which I find most effective. For this configuration you need twelve quartz crystals; two larger ones weighing between 0.5 and 1 kilogram (1lb and 2lb) each and the remaining ten should be at least 7.5 cm (3 inches) long and about 4 cm (1½ inches) wide.

Lie the patient on his or her back and make sure that they are perfectly comfortable. Place one of the larger crystals at the patient's head with the single-terminated end facing away from the body. The other large crystal should be placed at the feet with the single-terminated end facing upwards towards the body.

The other ten quartz crystals are placed around the body, five on each side, with their single-terminated ends facing upwards towards the head; one by the ankles, one by the knees, one by the hands, one by the elbows and one by the shoulders, on both sides of the body (see Plate x).

A thirteenth, or control, quartz crystal (I usually use my laser wand) is then passed over the other twelve quartz crystals by the healer in a clockwise direction, to create a unified magnetic energy field around the patient. The patient should lie in this position — cocooned in a 'sea' of crystal healing energy — for a period of between 15–20 minutes. The twelve-crystal configuration is used for balancing and harmonising the whole body.

Whilst the patient is receiving the full benefit of the crystal healing energies I usually do a complete 'aura-scan' of the body. I start at the head, placing my hands about 15 cm (6 inches) up from the body and slowly cover the whole body, using my hands as 'sensors'. Whenever I detect a possible imbalance, negative blockage or energy blockage my hands go red hot!

Having made a mental note of where the blockages exist I then move my control crystal in an anti-clockwise direction over the affected areas. This has the effect of clearing the blockage and neutralising any negativity that may have existed previously. In using the twelve-figure crystal configuration I have found that all my patients have experienced a profound metamorphosis by the time their healing session has ended. An inner depth of beautiful peace and tranquility is achieved and, at the right time and in the proper manner, it is possible to trigger an emotional release of stress and tension, the power of which is almost impossible to describe.

During all my workshops and seminars, when demonstrating the twelve-crystal configuration, I request that a volunteer steps forward to receive this treatment. Usually the person volunteering is exactly the right person upon whom to demonstrate as they are in urgent need of treatment. It is an interesting fact that a large percentage of the people attending my workshops and seminars do so out of a desire to receive crystal healing as much as to learn the techniques which I am discussing and demonstrating!

The energy and power created in a typical workshop or seminar is quite remarkable and helps greatly when it comes to focusing the love and healing energy necessary upon the volunteer. Very often this person experiences a profound release of emotional tension, negative blockages are removed and a great change comes over them. Sometimes I have to give them additional healing and counselling, in private, afterwards so that they may be led to release all that they need to. Crystal healing through configurations works upon all the subtle energies of the body and brings to the surface all the pent-up emotions and feelings of many years.

One elderly lady, in her mid-seventies, hobbled into my healing room accompanied by her sister. She had been unable to walk properly for the previous 14 years. I helped her up onto my massage couch and she lay down on her back. However, her left leg would not lie flat and she could only manage to have the knee 'arched' up in the air.

I placed the twelve crystals around her body and unified the magnetic energy field with my control crystal. Within 5 minutes her leg slowly began to move back down to lie flat on the couch. Her sister's mouth opened in astonishment. By the time the healing session had finished — after about another 20 minutes — she was a completely different person. She walked out of my healing room in a way which she would never have believed possible! She telephones me from time to time and her leg is still improving.

The Star of David Configuration

The Star of David is another very effective type of crystal configuration. The patient should sit on the floor, in yoga fashion, holding a crystal in the palm of their hand. Six quartz crystals are then placed around them in the form of a six-pointed star (see Figures 3 and 4).

Figure 3 Star of David crystal configuration. The patient sits in the middle, in yoga fashion, holding a crystal in the palm of the hand.

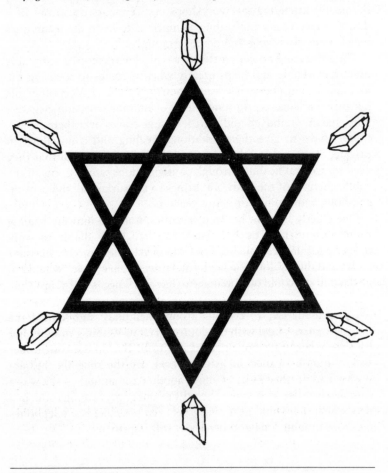

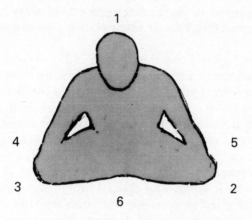

Figure 4

The two major points of the configuration in Figure 4, (1) behind the back and (6) in front of the feet when the patient is sitting in the lotus position, symbolise the balancing point between the spiritual at the back, and the physical at the front. These are the two crystals involved in the repolarisation and balance of vibrations within the patient. The crystals on the sides, closest to the back (4 and 5), are the other points of the physical trinity. The crystals closest to the legs (2 and 3), are the other points relating to the spiritual trinity.

The two crystals on the left side (2 and 5), relate to the lower half of the body, from the waist down, both spiritually and physically. The two crystals on the right side (3 and 4), relate to the upper half of the body, both spiritually and physically.

The Star of David crystal configuration enables you to cover all aspects of the patient's being and to correct the energy flows relating to the spiritual and the physical throughout the body. If the patient is suffering from any form of serious physical ailment then I suggest that you use your largest crystal in position 6, in the triangle relating to the physical. By doing this there will be a greater flow of energy to heal the physical vibrations. If the patient is in fairly good health, and the main purpose of the healing session is to treat spiritual or emotional stress then I would advise placing your largest crystal in position 1.

The seventh quartz crystal in the Star of David configuration is called the 'generator' and should be held in the hands of the person receiving the healing. It acts as the receiver of the energies that will be dispersed to the six surrounding crystals, to unify the magnetic energy field and to allow the body to draw what it needs from the flow of energy. Every crystal healer should acquire one quartz crystal to be used as a 'generator' crystal, and for no other purpose. In this way, their 'generator' will develop into an extension of their own energy pattern. It will become charged with their energies and will become more effective in healing treatments the more they use it!

The Star of David crystal configuration can also be used effectively with the patient lying on his or her back. One crystal should be placed at the head with the single-terminated end pointing away from the body. Two crystals should be placed at the knees, point upwards.

The crystal healer, as above, should take his personal healing crystal and energise the six crystals surrounding the patient's body by passing his crystal over all six quartz crystals. The patient should then lie within this healing field of crystal energy for a further 15–20 minutes.

Configurations for Special Ailments

For broken bones I would suggest that you use two single-terminated crystals. Place one below the fracture and one above the fracture with the points facing each other. This will speed up the healing process once the bones have been set properly by a qualified doctor and will also decrease the chance of infection and complications. The patient may also have a twelve-figure crystal configuration placed around him at the same time! For burns you should use the same treatment as for broken bones. You may also hold a third crystal over the burn area which will help to speed up the formation of new skin.

For hearing problems, use three single-terminated crystals: one at the top of the head, pointing down, and the other two behind the ears in the mastoid area, pointing inwards.

For spinal disorders the patient should lie on the floor, face downwards. Place a single-terminated quartz crystal between the ankles, pointing upwards towards the base of the spine. Place one crystal with the point downwards over the afflicted area of the spine. You do not want the energy to travel the total distance of the spine, only to the afflicted area.

For sprains in the ankle place a single quartz crystal on the foot, with the point on the ball of the foot. Hold another single quartz crystal, pointing down, at the knee. If the sprain is in the wrist, hold one crystal in the hand with the point upwards and the other at the shoulder with the point downwards. If the sprain is at the knee, place one crystal on the ball of the foot and the other crystal at the hip with the point downwards.

Migraine headaches are basically caused through the imbalance of energy flows throughout the physical body. To treat migraine I would use four single-terminated quartz crystals; one on each side of the neck between the neck and the collar bone with the points facing downwards. The patient should be lying down, face upwards. The two other quartz crystals should be positioned so as to lean against the balls of the feet with the points upwards. This will balance the energy flow through the main meridians.

Triangulations

In addition to the splendid crystal configurations I also use various forms of crystal 'triangulations'. Triangulations are basically three quartz crystals forming a triangular concentration of crystal energy on a specific part of the patient's body.

For example, lie your patient on his or her back. To treat upper body health conditions, place two crystals, one on each shoulder, points downwards, and a single crystal just below the navel with its point upwards. This will complete a triangulation of crystal energy in the upper part of the patient's body.

For lower body health conditions, place a single crystal, point downwards, just above the navel and two other quartz crystals, one on each thigh, points facing upwards. This will create a triangulation of crystal energy concentrated on the lower part of the patient's body. You may, of course, devise your own specific triangulations to meet the particular needs of your patient. Be flexible.

Triangulations with the patient sitting in a chair are often very powerful. For healing of the physical body place one quartz crystal in front of the chair with the single-terminated end facing away from the patient and two quartz crystals, one at either side of the chair and behind it, with their points facing towards the patient. For healing of the spiritual part of the body, place one quartz crystal behind the chair, with its single-terminated end facing away from the patient and two other quartz crystals, one at either side, in front of the chair, with their points directed towards the patient.

Whilst the patient is sitting in the chair in either of the above two triangulations, the crystal healer should pick up his personal quartz crystal and pass this crystal, in a circular clockwise motion, over the patient and the three quartz crystals encompassing the chair, in order to create a unified magnetic crystal energy field surrounding the body.

There are many different types of configurations, which may be used very successfully to help sort out many serious problems, including problems in relationships — whether that relationship is to wife, husband, lover, boyfriend, girlfriend or just simply a friend. If two people are in conflict with each other, perhaps out of stress, misunderstanding, or with their emotions, I strongly recommend a pattern of 'double triangulation' quartz crystals. This pattern will help create an understanding between the two and thus serves to create a balance between the flow of their vibrations.

The two individuals should sit facing each other, approximately 1 metre (3 feet) apart, in the lotus position (see Figure 5). Each should take two crystals and place them in a line behind themselves. They should then place a third quartz crystal in a position that forms a tirangle with the other quartz crystals, in front of them, with the single-terminated end facing the other person. Draw an imaginary line at the mid-point between the two people. The pointer crystal should be over that line, into the area of the other person. This will serve to interlock both triangles and form an invisible diamond in the centre where the two triangles intercept each other.

The effect you are creating is a symbolic one. You are taking the energies of the trinity of one, and blending them with the energies of the trinity of the other. The results will be healing and releasing, and creating an understanding between the two.

This pattern of configurations is extremely effective when utilised by two individualis whose spiritual vibrations are closely aligned as it will unite them even closer! It might also be effective when utilised between a parent and a child, to create a more peaceful and understanding relationship between them.

Figure 5　A crystal configuration which helps two individuals to understand each other and to resolve any conflicts in their relationship.

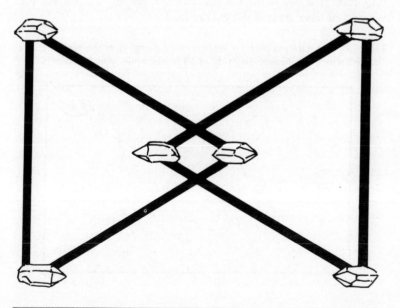

Bed Patterns

Bed patterns are a form of triangulation which establishes an energy force-field whilst the patient is asleep in his or her bed at night, which heals, energises, builds resistance to outside negativity and ensures a very peaceful period of relaxation and rest.

The quartz crystals should be placed between the mattress and the box spring, taped to the frame of a water bed or placed on the floor under the bed. One crystal should be put at the top centre of the bed, with its single-terminated end facing inwards, the other two should be placed at the foot of the bed. The point of all three crystals must face the centre of the bed (see Figure 6).

The bed pattern creates a triangle of concentrated crystal energy to rest and sleep within. The field of crystal energy will gradually spread out until the entire bed becomes a force-field. Throughout the night, while the patient is asleep, gentle crystal energies penetrate the body at all levels, thus helping to restore the patient to full health.

Whenever positioning the crystals to form a bed pattern it is important that you affirm the desired end result and the purpose for which you have created the energy field.

Figure 6 Bed patterns create a 'sea' of crystal energy over the whole area of the bed which penetrates the body at all levels whilst you are asleep.

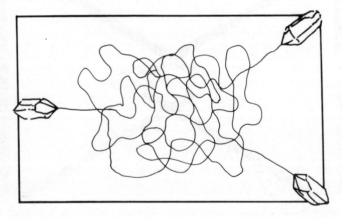

Room Patterns

Room patterns create an energy field to maintain positive vibrations, remove all negativity and to strengthen your energies each day. Position one quartz crystal in each corner of the room, with their single-terminated ends facing into the centre of the room (see Figure 7). These may be placed on the floor or fixed to the ceiling.

The quartz crystals must be left in place at all times to have the maximum effect. You will find that they will generate a field of pure positive energy, allowing you to remain free of unwanted negative energies that your clients, friends and visitors may unconsciously emit. As with the bed patterns, whenever placing the crystals to form a room pattern, it is important that you affirm the desired end result and the purpose for which you have created the energy field. This will ensure that you do not take on any negative energy from others.

Figure 7   Room patterns ensure that the room is completely 'energised' with positive pure crystalline energy.

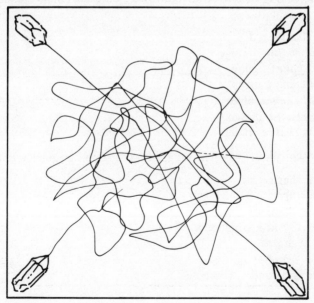

14

The Total Healing Experience

The total healing experience involves bringing together a combination of crystals, colour and sound to make a perfect trinity. At present we have researchers into colour therapy, researchers into sound therapy and, of course, people like myself who are researching crystal healing techniques. In the fullness of time I anticipate that all three areas will begin to merge into one cohesive unit.

Very simply each *chakra* vibrates on a different colour frequency, thus:

Base chakra red
Sexual chakra orange
Solar chakra yellow
Heart chakra green
Throat chakra blue
Brow chakra indigo
Crown chakra violet

And each colour 'vibrates' on a different sound frequency, thus:

Red F sharp
Orange B flat
Yellow G major
Green C and E combined
Blue D sharp
Indigo A minor
Violet B, D and G combined

All the quartz crystals used in configurations should be bathed in the colour associated with the area of the disease, and by evoking the vibrations of the relevant sound or note, at the same time, a complete harmony of vibrations will be created that is in total compatibility with the organic structure.

Some researchers — especially in the field of complementary medicine — have been experimenting for many years with the effects of colour and colour therapy upon the human form. Recently they have also become interested in sound. I believe that the time is fast approaching when we shall be able to expand our crystal consciousness and knowledge, here in the twentieth century, in a way that few people have dared to dream so far.

The Crystal Rescue Remedy

One of the first students to pass the Crystal Healing Certificated Course run by the Crystal Research Foundation was Dennis West, M. Crys.H. The Crystal Rescue Remedy was 'channelled' through Dennis in trance guidance and has proven very effective in calming the fears and anxieties of many people. It is taken internally to relieve stress and brings together the subtle healing energies of specially selected crystals and gemstones whose healing vibrations are brought together for the specific purposes of balancing, harmonising and calming the mind and emotional systems of the body.

The Crystal Rescue Remedy will be found to be especially useful as an aid to absorbing the shock of traumatic experience, and helps give strength to those suffering the loss of a loved one. It will help calm those who suffer from stage fright, or are about to take a driving test, interviews, or examinations of any kind. The remedy will be found to be a friend in almost all situations where the mind and emotions need to be calmed and strengthened.

Two or three drops of the Crystal Rescue Remedy should be taken, on or under the tongue, when needed. Three or four drops may also be taken in a wine glass of water. Where the cause of emotional stress is prolonged such as in a bereavement) it will be found helpful to take two or three drops of the remedy in each warm drink, including tea and coffee, until the heart and mind are once more at peace.

The Crystal Rescue Remedy is absolutely safe and accidental overdose can do no harm whatsoever.

15

Colour Crystal Healing

For our colour crystal healing we have designed our own crystal light box which is a rectangular or square box with a hole in the centre for a small light bulb. Colour filters — or gels — are placed over the hole where the light shines up through the box. Light box quartz crystals are placed over the filters. When crystals are used in this way they intensify and project colour rays into the environment that may be used for healing and upliftment.

Light box crystals can either be flat-based, single generator crystals, or clusters. The only requirement for a light box crystal is the capability of reflecting light from the base up through the entire crystal.

For many thousands of years, from the days of Atlantis and beyond, to the present generation, colour and colour rays have been used for the purposes of healing. Colour impinges on every waking moment and even penetrates our dreams. Everywhere around us in our world, everything we use or wear or see, is coloured. So what is colour?

Many people have quite definite ideas and feelings about colour. The love of colour springs from the individual's inner consciousness. Colour affects us emotionally, making things warm or cold, provocative or sympathetic, exciting or tranquil. Some people are far more sensitive to colour than others and are attracted, even fascinated, and thrilled, by certain colours; others may be repelled or seem quite unaffected by the same colour vibrations. It is apparent therefore that colour exerts a very powerful influence upon our minds and emotions. Colour is not a lifeless, static phenomenon, as many people suppose, but a vital force, a strong influence on all our lives!

Colour is an important tool, though few people see it as such, or think about how it can be 'managed'. However, colour consultants 'manage' colour when they awaken interest and increase productivity with a thoughtful colour scheme for a factory or office, create moods with restaurant lighting schemes or make quiet diesel locomotives more visible at level crossings. Colour management can include designing sleep-inducing colour schemes for bedrooms, or dressing children in colours that stand out against dull streets, and, in poor lighting conditions, reduce the risk of accidents in the street. Some psychologists are even able to analyse individuals from the way they choose and use colour.

Colour is an interface between us and the world, although insufficient education in colour makes most people's handling of it something of a hit-and-miss affair. Many people use colour impressively in their dress, yet their homes may indicate neither taste nor courage, because they do not understand colour. People dress once or twice a day but decorate, on average, bi-annually. Yet it is the colour around them that most affects their moods and personality.

Knowledge, judgement and intuition are all combined in the capable management of colour, which is a disicpline and an art. Among the rewards of its mastery are a greater sensitivity to the medium of colour and increased satisfaction from its handling. Knowing how colours are named and standardised, how they change under different kinds of lighting, why they fade, how they can be used to alter mood, line, form, shape and perspective and understanding the optical effects of certain colour combinations and the psychological impact of coloured lighting — all are essential if you are to succeed in making colour do what you want it to!

There is an ancient and widespread faith in the healing power of colour and that this power can be used to heal imbalances of both mind and body. How great, then, must be this power when combined with the might and energy of the quartz crystal?

Gemstones, seemingly filled with coloured light of a peculiarly mystical kind, have always been held in reverence and in ancient times were ground and diluted, or dipped in water, to be used as remedies for all diseases. Yellow beryls, for example, were used to cure jaundice; bloodstones treated haemorrhage and disorders of the blood; and the prismatic diamond was considered a cure-all, as is the quartz crystal today.

Colour exists on all planes of life, as vibrations are everywhere and colour is a manifestation of vibration. The universal light, the sun, emanates vibratory streams of life-force in seven major rays. Each individual is believed to incarnate into their own specific colour, which is the major ray, and this contains their own individual shade of degree of evolution. Everybody also possesses three other rays, known as the minor rays, which are the soul colours. When all these rays are in harmony with each other, the individual will enjoy good health and abundant energy. When the rays are not in harmony, however, energy levels will decrease and sickness will occur. It is at this time that the living energy of both colour and crystals can be used to create, restore and renew.

Every colour has positive and negative tones. Clear, strong tones of a colour in the aura indicate the positive qualities: application, force and will. Weak, faded or dull tones in the aura indicate lack of force and instability. Some colours are warming: red, orange and yellow; some are cooling: blue, violet and magenta; whilst green, the middle or balancing colour is neutral.

The more light that a person attracts to him or herself, through spiritual living and high ideals, the more beautiful will be the colours of his or her aura. The highly evolved person will have only positive tones, properly balanced and controlled. He will appear to be surrounded by rays of light which will be soothing and healing to others.

In the aura of the less evolved man, the colours will be less pure and luminous. The auric colours may be clouded, dull and unpleasant to see — there may even be 'clouds', 'flecks' or even 'holes' in the aura. One can usually intuitively tell if the reasons for these imbalances are due to stress, illness, weakness, or the taking of chemical drugs, or alcohol, smoking, or poor nutrition.

The seven major *chakras*, or energy centres, are all 'keyed' to the seven colours of the spectrum (see p. 82).

Imbalances in one *chakra*, or more, will affect the whole being.

Healing can be effected in many different ways, but there are two principal methods of applying colour crystal therapy; either by the application of colour to a part of, or the whole of, the body, with beams of light shone through coloured filters and amplified by the use of a light box quartz crystal, or by the use of gemstones according to their individual colours.

The first method requires the acquisition of a crystal light box. These can be supplied by The Crystal Research Foundation or if you are a do-it-yourself enthusiast you may, of course, construct your own (see p. 85).

The most practical form of light box is one that is small and easily portable. The bulb should be a full spectrum daylight blue, giving the same effect as natural daylight, and on no account should you ever use an ultra-violet bulb. The light box should be constructed so that the light is reflected through the opening, which can be either at the front or on top of the box.

It is very important that your light box should be made in such a way that the filters or gels can be changed quietly and easily without disturbing the patient or burning the therapist. It should also be properly ventilated so that no heat is felt by the patient: the object of the exercise is light, not heat! Treatment will be made much easier if the light box could be mounted on a stand so that it can be tilted easily to various angles, or raised or lowered.

The most important part of the crystal light box is the filters and, if possible, only hand-crafted stained glass should be used. This will have a density and vibration which cannot be manufactured artificially but, like any natural matter from mother earth, can be cleansed and dedicated to your purpose and all traces of negativity removed.

The glow of stained glass is as much the result of bubbles and impurities as anything else, and the light is not merely admitted, but held, giving a luminous, jewel-like quality. Each filter made from hand-crafted stained glass, no matter what colour it appears to be, will contain the entire spectrum of colours within it, and its properties are truly magical. The glaziers working with stained glass today are visionary artists on a grand scale; their raw material is daylight, the visible manifestation of God in creation, which they can translate with glass into vibrant colour.

Only five basic colour filters need to be obtained: red, yellow, green, violet and blue, as the following colours can be created from these combinations:

Red and Yellow = Orange   Red and Violet* = Magenta
Blue and Violet = Indigo   Magenta and Red = Scarlet
Yellow and Green = Lemon   Blue and Red = Scarlet
Blue and Green = Turquoise

* Violet gives a very low luminosity, so try to obtain a separate filter of magenta.

For general colour crystal healing treatments, the best crystal to use is quartz, and this should be placed on top of the coloured filter so that the light then directed to the patient shines through the filter and through the crystal.

Quartz has the widest energy spectrum of the more common crystals, and makes up approximately 30 per cent of the earth's crust, and for these reasons is most likely to be compatible with the patient. Quartz crystal is also very easy to work with, and, for the most part, has a very appealing clarity.

I find it best to keep one special quartz light box crystal for all work using colour crystal healing. Always cleanse this crystal between patients. If a light box crystal has been used on the light box with a particular colour, and you wish to use it with another colour, it is best to cleanse the crystal first.

The choice of colour that you use in your treatment session will greatly depend on your study of the patient and his or her symptoms. Usually you will have discovered that one or more of the *chakra* centres is out of balance and you will need to treat the appropriate *chakra* or *chakras* in order to restore harmony to the body. I find that my electro-crystal scanner is a very accurate and effective way to ascertain which *chakras* need treatment, but never underestimate your intuitive faculties.

The following is only meant as a general guide to the application of some of the colours:

Red This is the most powerful colour and it should, therefore, be used carefully. It is revitalising, stimulating and arousing; it promotes inhalation and raises the blood pressure. It can be useful in treating chronic diseases, and helps with rheumatism and arthritis (sacral gland).

Orange This is an anti-depressant colour, promotes good digestion and is beneficial to most of the metabolic system; it increases oxygen and so helps the lungs function properly. It can draw boils, and brings abscesses to a head. It is rejuvenating, but can also raise blood pressure (adrenals).

Yellow This colour can stimulate the nervous system, help with mental illness and also stimulate the lymphatic glands. It may help with the treatment of arthritis by removing density deposits in the body (solar plexus).

Green Just like red, this colour must be used carefully. Although it is the ray of balance, overuse can promote the dissolving of virgin cell structure and also original cells. It stimulates the pituitary, raises the vibrations, and is very beneficial for minor cuts, sores and bruises. It is the colour to use in the treatment of cancer, but it must *never* be used on a woman who is pregnant (thymus).

Turquoise Refreshing and cooling, turquoise is restful for a nervous person and also helps inflammation. It is good, too, for eczema.

Blue Of all the colours this is the most healing. The colour blue promotes exhalation and reduces blood pressure. It is the light of peace, relaxing the whole body, and regulating the harmonious development of tissue and body structure. It removes headaches and migraines, and is also useful in cases of asthma. It aids sleep, reduces fear, soothes infections and inflammations, and relieves itches and burns (thyroid).

Violet In this colour two effects meet; the relaxing in the blue and the stimulating in the red. It is the colour of a consciousness balance — the colour of divinity, creativity and also stability. It will raise the self-esteem of an individual who has lost the sense of human beauty, and restore rhythm to the system (pituitary).

Magenta This colour draws an individual into spiritual awareness. It should be used only rarely and is usually a colour for a more mature person (pineal).

It is also important to note that each colour has an emotional and mental quality which should be taken into account when treating your patient as the psychological condition often affects the physical.

Red energy		**Turquoise** immunity	
Orange joy		**Blue** relaxing	
Yellow detachment		**Violet** dignity/self-respect	
Green balance/equilibrium		**Magenta** dissolving/letting go.	

One very important colour which has not yet been mentioned is pink, the colour usually associated with love, the emotions, and particularly with mother-love. The colour pink has a calming effect on the emotional level and helps people suffering from emotional traumas or problems with their relationships.

Gemstones in Colour Crystal Healing

Gemstones are used by some crystal healers in colour crystal therapy because they are of one pure colour, unmixed and unadulterated in effect, and the rays are concentrated within the gemstones themselves. One theory accounting for their effectiveness is that the planets influence human behaviour physically, psychologically, emotionally and spiritually, and since the gemstones possess the same rays as the planets, they also possess the same, slightly less forceful, influences as the planets.

The true colour of a gemstone is revealed by the use of the prism. For example, the rays of a diamond are seen as white by the naked eye, but are indigo when seen under the prism. Therefore, indigo is the true colour of the diamond.

The following table encapsulates Indian medicine and may be a useful guide.

Day	Taste	Planet	Gem	Colour	Element	Symbol	Polarity
Sunday	Pungent	Sun	Ruby	Red	Fire	R	Negative
Monday	Astringent	Moon	Pearl	Orange	Water	O	Positive
Tuesday	Bitter	Mars	Coral	Yellow	Fire	Y	Negative
Wednesday	All Tastes	Mercury	Emerald	Green	Water	S	Positive
Thursday	Sweet	Jupiter	Moonstone	Blue	Air	B	Neutral
Friday	Sour	Venus	Diamond	Indigo	Water	I	Positive
Saturday	Saline	Saturn	Sapphire	Violet	Air	V	Neutral

The use of gemstones according to their particular colours can, on some occasions, be a little confusing, as many gemstones have healing properties which do not appear to correspond with the colour of their particular centre in the body! If I recommend that a patient wears or carries a particular stone around with them, my suggestion may have been made on the basis of its colour, or alternatively for its inherent healing properties and in some cases they may not match. Take some green stones, for example. The emerald is said to improve the intellect and memory and help cure insomnia, while malachite helps asthma, toothache and irregular periods and improves the eyesight, and so on.

The key to the problem is more subtle: all the symptoms listed above are purely physical manifestations of an imbalance in the soul. So look at your patient, and try to determine *why* they are manifesting a damaged kidney or skin rash. What is the psychological cause for it? If the indication for treatment is a gemstone which happens to be green look at what is happening in the patient's heart *chakra*! My advice at all times is to use your intuition if you are not sure what to do!

One colour crystal therapist told me whenever he is feeling lethargic or lacks energy he places a yellow filter on his light box, 'programmes' his light box crystal accordingly and sits in front of the crystal light box for 15 minutes. He says that this short treatment is enough to give him energy to work half the night!

Colour crystal healing may either be used as a therapy in its own right or in conjunction with another major therapy (e.g. acupuncture). It is undoubtedly a very powerful and effective therapeutic healing 'tool', which may be used by therapists anywhere, at any time, to bring help and relief to those in their care. During the past couple of years we have distributed crystal light boxes to therapists representing all the major natural health therapies; acupuncturists, osteopaths, hypnotherapists, herbalists, masseurs, homoeopaths and reflexologists.

16

Gem Elixirs

Gem elixirs are prepared from natural gemstones and minerals; and each elixir possesses the pure essence of the gemstone itself, combining energy, colour and vibration in the form of a liquid. These elixirs have absolutely no harmful side effects.

Gem elixirs work upon the subtle energies of the body at all levels. The vibrations and natural energies of each individual gemstone are channelled into the gem elixir, which can then be used to treat many health conditions. Up to seven drops of the gem elixir is recommended as a normal dosage and, for best results, these should be taken three times a day; upon waking in the morning, at noon and before retiring to bed in the evening. In acute cases, however, the elixir may be taken every hour.

Once a gem elixir has been ingested, it follows a specific path through the physical and subtle bodies, initially being assimilated into the circulation system. It then settles midway between the circulatory and nervous systems, where an electro-magnetic current is created by the polarity of these two systems. From there the elixir usually moves directly to the meridians, and then enters the various subtle bodies, the *chakras*, or returns directly to the physical level. The elixir's path is determined by the type of elixir being used and the kind of person using it.

The gem elixir can usually be taken for three to four weeks at a time. Response rate can vary from the first few minutes to many weeks, depending upon the patient's sensitivity. Various practices, such as meditation and creative visualisation, while not essential, can positively influence the effects of the elixir.

All gem elixirs are placed under a pyramid surrounded by quartz crystals and loadstones for increased amplification. They are stored in a 2.5 metre (8-foot) gold-plated pyramid with a 24-carat gold capstone.

Gem elixirs seem to work best when they are used in combinations for specific requirements. For combinations, drops from individual bottles containing gem elixirs may be taken at the same time, but there is a greatly amplified effect if larger equal amounts from individual gem elixir bottles are poured into an empty bottle and then taken gradually.

All gem elixars are self-adjusting, so they are very safe. On rare occasions one can detoxify too rapidly with gem elixirs and, in such cases, all one needs to do is to lessen the dosage for a short period.

The following gem elixirs are generally available:

Abalone This is an excellent elixir for treating spinal degeneration disease and strengthening the heart.

Agate (Botswana) This elixir is particularly effective in high-pressure oxygen therapies, used to treat tumours, neurological and skin tissue regeneration and lung damage.

Agate (Carnelian) This is used to treat anorexia nervosa.

Agate (Fire) This elixir influences the entire endocrine system and restimulates the memory cells.

Agate (Moss) This agate elixir can ease lymphomas, Hodgkin's disease and diabetes. It can also be used to ease allergies and for kidney disorders and liver problems.

Alexandrite Has an impact on the nervous system, spleen and pancreas. Central nervous system diseases, leukaemia, and disorders associated with the lymph gland and spleen are alleviated. Low self-esteem and difficulty in centering the self are important clues to the need for this elixir.

Amazonite The activities of the heart and solar plexus *chakras* are aligned, which also aligns the etheric mental bodies. This elixir has very important ethereal properties.

Amber Strengthens the thyroid and inner ear. People needing amber may exhibit memory loss, inability to make decisions, eccentric behaviour and anxiety.

Amethyst Calms patient in stressful situations, allows clarity of thought and is good for headaches and migraines. Gives confidence, stimulates patients who lack vision and helps greater attunement with God.

Aquamarine Reduces fear and anxiety, and an inability to express oneself. Excellent for all throat and upper chest conditions.

Aventurine Alleviates psychosomatic illness, anxiety and buried fears, particularly those that originated during the first seven years of childhood. This elixir helps develop more emotional tranquility and a more positive attitude to life.

Azurite This is particularly effective in the treatment of diseases of the bone such as arthritis and spinal curvature.

Azurite with Malachite This elixir has an impact upon the liver, skin, thymus, muscular dystrophy and cirrhosis of the liver.

Beryl Used for the intestinal tract, the cardiovascular system and hardening of the arteries. The over-analytical or critical person could do with this elixir.

Bloodstone Assists the bone marrow, spleen, heart, testicles, ovaries, cervix and uterus. Spiritually, this elixir generates a higher state of consciousness.

Brass Eliminates toxins throughout the body, stimulates hair growth, aligns the vertebrae and helps scalp and skin diseases.

Bronze Helps produce red corpuscles, which may ease leukaemia.

Calcite This elixir increases the mental capacity for astral projection.

Chalcedony Stimulates bone marrow and increases the production of red corpuscles.

Chrysocolla Strengthens the lungs, thyroid and coccyx. Stress and hypertension are eased and emotions are balanced. Use this elixir when doing breathing exercises for more control over spiritual forces. Chrysocolla amplifies the throat *chakra*.

Chrysoprase The primary focus of this elixir is upon the prostate gland, testicles, Fallopian tubes and the ovaries.

Citrine Removes toxins from the lower area of the body.

Copper Can be used in a wide range of inflammatory conditions such as arthritis, inner ear and intestinal disorders. It strengthens the pineal and pituitary glands and aligns the five lower *chakras*.

Coral Balances the entire personality; use for emotional calm, attunement to nature and to increase expressive abilities and creativity. All meridians and etheric bodies are balanced.

Diamond This elixir is extremely effective in removing negative blockages which interfere with vibrational remedies. It removes blockages in the personality, and is used in cases of anxiety and insecurity.

Emerald Balances the heart *chakra*, stimulates the meridian points, balances the emotions, strengthens will-power and improves the memory.

Fluorite Strengthens the teeth, eases bone tissue and dental disease. In a mouthwash this elixir helps prevent tooth decay.

Garnet Stimulates the first *chakra*. People who are self-centred should have this elixir.

Gold This elixir is the great balancer of the heart *chakra*, critical to the circulatory flows of the body. It is the master healer, aligns higher spiritual thoughts and increases the ability to give and receive love.

Haematite Helps the blood-cleansing function of the kidneys.

Herkimer Diamond This elixir releases stress and tension, and in particular the type of stress that leads to malignant tumours. Similar to the diamond, the herkimer radiates energy.

Jade Helps the individual to become more articulate. Gives courage, wisdom, sensitivity and increases psychic ability.

Jasper (Green) This elixir is used to promote healing on all levels, and aligns intuitive forces.

Lapis Lazuli This elixir is effective in treating tonsilitis. Its impact extends to the larynx and bronchial passages. It releases buried emotions and anxieties, and improves meditation.

Loadstone (Negative and Positive) Increases the biomagnetic forces in the body, and can be used in magnetic healing. This elixir makes the aura more sensitive and strengthens it and balances the male and female.

Magnetite Stimulates the entire endocrine system. Aligns *chakras* and stimulates deeper meditation.

Malachite Assists in correcting irregular menstruation, increases fertility and reduces stomach ulcers.

Meteorite This is a very important elixir, and can be taken at any

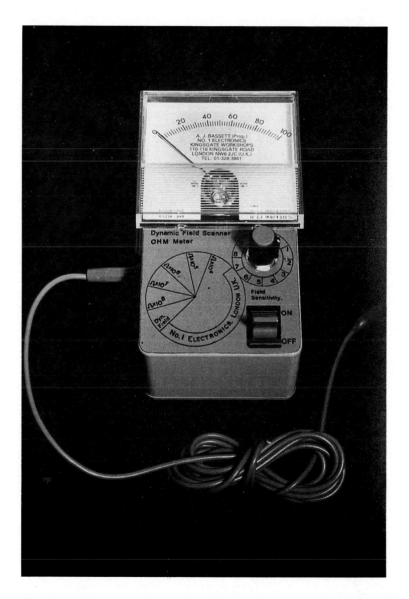

Plate 1   An electro-crystal scanning meter

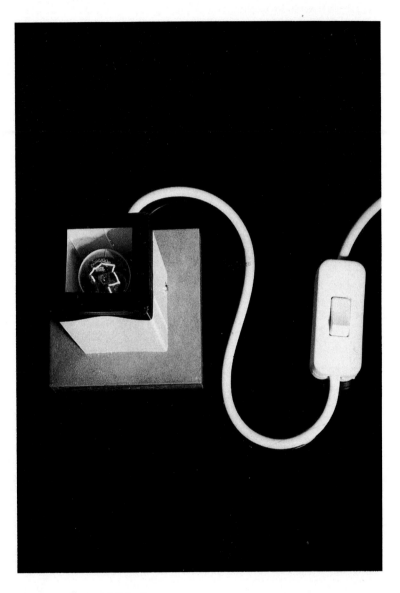

Plate 11 A crystal light box

Plate III   A quartz crystal cluster

Plate IV   An amethyst cluster

Plate v   A Nigerian quartz crystal

Plate VI A blue quartz sphere

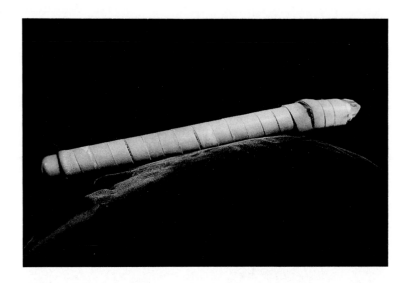

Plate VII   A crystal wand

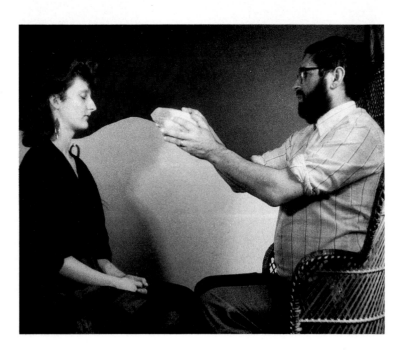

Plate VIII   Crystal hypnosis

Plate IX Crystal triangulation

Plate X   A crystal healing configuration

Plate XI   Crystal massage

time. Protects against planetary radiation, ley lines and geopathic stress (created by a convergence of negative ley lines) and is also good for protecting the aura.

Moonstone Helps to control emotions, particularly those that cause anxiety and stress. It is a female stone, and the elixir should be used for pelvic disorders.

Obsidian Balances the intestine and muscle tissue in the stomach area.

Onyx Regenerates the heart, kidney and nerve tissue.

Opal (Dark) This variety of opal elixir affects the ovaries, testicles, pancreas, helps release depression and acts as a grounding element for the emotional body. The thought force is amplified.

Opal (Light) Helps ease autism, dyslexia, epilepsy and visual problems. Helps the patient to seek for higher inspiration.

Pearl This is a powerful elixir which alleviates all emotional imbalances. Emotional stress affects the stomach and lower back, and can manifest itself in other stress-related diseases.

Peridot Helps to remove gradually all toxicity in the body, gives a more positive emotional outlook on life, and increases patience.

Platinum Reduces arrogance, depression, pride, stress and memory loss from shock or tragedy.

Pyrite This elixir is a digestive aid for the abdomen and upper intestine, and aids the production of enzymes.

Quartz (Smoky) Helps sexual problems in both sexes, and aids proper release of the *Kundalini* energy. Meditation with smoky quartz removes unclear thought forms.

Quartz (White) Amplifies the crystalline properties in the body, alleviates emotional extremes, improves assimilation of the amino acids. The emotional and etheric bodies are aligned. The third eye, head and solar plexus *chakra*s are also aligned.

Rhodocrosite Helps to detoxify the kidneys. There is a general strengthening of self-identity and ability to function better in life.

Rhodonite This elixir strengthens the inner ear bone tissue and sense of hearing.

Rose Quartz Helps overcome emotional problems, like anger or tension. Increases confidence and negates false pride. Balances the emotions and stimulates the heart *chakra*.

Ruby Acts upon the first *chakra*, which in turn affects the heart, activates the *Kundalini*, creates balance in spiritual endeavours and amplifies thought power.

Rutile Tends to reverse ageing disorders associated with a poor immune system. Stimulates inactive or unused parts of the brain. Increases clairvoyance and develops inspiration.

Sapphire Aligns the spinal column and improves communication with the higher sides of life. Links the mind, body and spirit to bring feeling of being at one.

Sardonyx Aids the lungs, larynx, thyroid and the nervous system.

Silver Stimulates the nerve tissue. Increases the IQ and stimulates the speech centres. Silver elixir is also used for mental imbalances such as schizophrenia.

Sodalite Strengthens the lymphatic system. Helps to attain emotional balance for the purpose of spiritual growth.

Spinel This elixir is a powerful general cleanser. Helps to detoxify the system.

Tigers Eye Works on the adrenal glands and cleanses the bowels and bladder areas.

Topaz Calms the passions, improves appetite, and is a source of strength when dealing with problems. Stimulates the third *chakra*, and helps to assimilate newly stabilised emotions.

Tourmaline (Black) Assists the first *chakra* and alleviates imbalances such as arthritis and adrenal disorders.

Tourmaline (Rubellite) Activates the qualities of the second *chakra*; for instance, creativity and fertility are stimulated.

Tourmaline (Clear) Activates the third *chakra* and helps problems associated with it (e.g. digestion, ulcers).

Tourmaline (Green) Opens the *chakras* and regenerates the heart, thymus and immune system.

Tourmaline (Blue) Activates the throat *chakra*, and strengthens the larynx, throat and thyroid.

Tourmaline (Cats-Eye) This is the elixir for the sixth *chakra*. It stimulates the endocrine system, and awakens personal concepts of God.

Tourmaline (Quartz) This elixir opens the head *chakra*. Aligns all subtle bodies (energy centres invisible to the naked eye) and *chakra*s, aids greater attunement to the higher self, and increases spiritual understanding.

Turquoise This elixir is a master healer: it strengthens the entire anatomy and protects the aura.

Zircon Merges the forces of the pineal and pituitary gland on a physical level and opens and balances the chakras associated with these two glands.

The following is a list of symptoms and the corresponding gem elixirs which may be useful in treatment:

Acidity pyrite
Acne moss agate, aventurine, fire agate
Addictions
    Alcohol amethyst, emerald, jade
    Tobacco gold
    Drugs emerald
Ageing gold, silver, copper
Anaemia all tourmalines, gold, garnet, magnetite
Appetite citrine, amethyst
Arthritis lapis lazuli, dark opal, clear quartz, ruby
Asthma pearl, tourmaline, cats-eye, amethyst, emerald
Backache amethyst
Bladder weakness loadstone, malachite, silver
Blood pressure
    High pearl, emerald
    Low ruby, magnetite
    Irregular ruby, pearl
Bronchitis pearl, azurite
Burns malachite, pearl, ruby, turquoise
Calcium excess chrysocolla
Cataract malachite, clear quartz, turquoise
Circulatory problems emerald, ruby, bloodstone, pearl
Cold hands and feet ruby, magnetite, haematite
Colds pearl
Colitis emerald
Colour-blindness amethyst
Constipation topaz, ruby

Convulsions copper, magnetite
Cough topaz, azurite
Cramps copper, malachite, moonstone
Croup topaz, diamond
Cysts spinel
Dandruff diamond
Deafness moonstone
Diabetes moss agate, loadstone, malachite, amethyst, rhodonite
Diarrhoea beryl, magnetite
Digestive problems coral onyx
Dizziness copper, loadstone, magnetite, malachite
Dysentery emerald, copper
Dyspepsia emerald, diamond
Earache diamond, fluorite, platinum, silver
Eczema sapphire, coral
Epilepsy copper, gold, silver, meteorite
Fatigue ruby, pearl, moonstone, emerald, diamond, rose quartz
Fever copper, coral, gold, jasper, ruby, silver
Fissure, anal diamond
Flatulence coral, emerald, topaz
Gallstones chalcedony, magnetite
Gastric ulcer emerald
Glands, swollen moonstone, aquamarine
Goitre topaz
Gout pearl, topaz, turquoise
Gums carnelian, coral
Haemorrhage pearl, all agates, garnet
Haemorrhoids coral, diamond
Hay fever pearl, topaz
Headaches haematite, loadstone, malachite, platinum, amethyst
Heart disease emerald, ruby
Heartburn chrysocolla
Hepatitis coral, citrine
Herpes aventurine, garnet
Hyperglycemia moss agate, amethyst
Hysteria coral, sodalite
Impotence magnetite, ruby, tourmaline, cats-eye

Indigestion coral, pearl
Infections malachite, obsidian, ruby, silver
Infertility
  Men pearl, amethyst, bloodstone
  Women malachite, rose quartz, ruby, loadstone
Inflammations bloodstone, pearl, ruby
Influenza topaz, moonstone, gold, fluorite, copper, beryl
Jaundice copper, coral, magnetite
Kidney stones amethyst, emerald, jade
Laryngitis lapis lazuli, pyrite
Leukaemia bloodstone, bronze, copper, diamond, obsidian, opal, ruby
Leprosy diamond, sapphire, tourmaline, cats-eye, onyx, fluorite
Liver infections lapis lazuli, opal, quartz, ruby, beryl, peridot
Lumbago loadstone, magnetite
Memory, poor emerald
Menstruation
  Irregular: tourmaline
  Heavy: sapphire
  Painful: lapis lazuli, opal, quartz, ruby
Meningitis pearl, sapphire
Menopause herkimer diamond, malachite
Mental debility topaz
Migraine amethyst, fluorite
Mouth infections jasper
Multiple Sclerosis gold
Mumps copper
Nails, strengthening graphite, sulphur
Nausea emerald, onyx, sapphire
Nervous exhaustion opal, pearl, quartz, silver
Nervous depression meteorite, copper, gold, silver
Neuralgia coral, amethyst, diamond
Numbness platinum
Obesity malachite, amethyst
Palpitation ruby, malachite
Pancreas infection magnetite, malachite, black tourmaline
Paralysis platinum

Parkinson's disease kunzite
Pharyngitis pyrite
Pneumonia opal, pearl, amethyst
Pregnancy nausea rubellite tourmaline, silver, amethyst
Pre-menstrual stress lapiz lazuli, opal, clear quartz, ruby
Prostate haematite
Psoriasis onyx, pearl
Rheumatism black tourmaline, sardonyx, malachite, loadstone,
    gold, chrysocolla
Scarlet fever copper
Sciatica copper
Schizophrenia meteorite, amethyst, rose quartz
Scleroma beryl, chalcedony
Sexual problems lapiz lazuli, dark opal, clear quartz, ruby
Shock meteorite, pearl, diamond
Spasms copper, jasper, amethyst, silver
Spermatorrhoea light opal, pearl
Sterility dark opal
Stomach troubles azurite, coral, opal, pearl, rose quartz
Syphilis malachite, pearl
Tonsilitis lapis lazuli, pyrite
Toxaemia positive and negative loadstone, clear quartz
Typhoid fever coral
Varicose veins copper, coral
Vertigo tourmaline, diamond
Vomiting coral, pearl
Water retention tourmaline, cats-eye
Weight problems lapis lazuli, malachite, turquoise

The following list of psychological problems and associated health
conditions may be treated with one or more gem elixirs:

Anger beryl, diamond, peridot
Anxiety stress amethyst, lapis lazuli, diamond, onyx, light pearl
Apathy copper, onyx, dark opal
Argumentativeness sulphur
Arrogance platinum
Carelessness lapis lazuli

Concentration, lack of diamond, onyx, light pearl
Courage, lack of jade, amethyst, sardonyx, sodalite
Depression beryl, lapis lazuli, limestone, amethyst, onyx
Disappointment ruby, platinum
Dreams diamond, clear and rose quartz, emerald, peridot
Emotional balance sodalite, garnet
Envy diamond, topaz
Excitedness copper, gold, jet, kunzite, platinum
Fear of ageing blue quartz
Fear of death copper
Fear of eating black tourmaline, rose quartz
Fear of relationships sodalite
Frustration lapis lazuli, dark opal, clear quartz, ruby
Greed chrysoprase
Grief ruby, sardonyx, white tourmaline
Grudges ruby, turquoise
Guilt chrysoprase, sodalite
Harmony, lack of fire agate, emerald, ruby, green tourmaline, gold
Hostility lapidolite
Humility, lack of sardonyx
Hyperactiveness graphite, sapphire, black tourmaline
Hysteria amethyst, emerald, jade
Imagination, lack of chrysoprase, garnet, silver, spinel
Inferiority complex gold
Inhibitions carbon, steel
Insecurity diamond
Insomnia emerald, clear quartz, peridot
Irritability beryl, lapis lazuli, limestone, sapphire
Laziness beryl
Lethargy light opal, pearl, tigers eye, topaz, coral, diamond
Memory amethyst, platinum, kunzite, copper, amber
Negativity all tourmalines
Nervous tension garnet, ruby, sapphire
Nightmares beryl, diamond, peridot, emerald, clear quartz, tigers
eye
Obsession emerald, rose quartz, tigers eye
Patience ruby, turquoise

Possessiveness quartzite
Pride, false platinum, rose quartz
Religious intolerance amethyst, lapis lazuli
Resentment coral
Responsibility, lack of gold
Rigidity all quartzes
Schizophrenia red coral, emerald, dark opal, light pearl, clear quartz
Sedation, in need of lapis lazuli, malachite, light pearl, turquoise, dark opal
Self-awareness, lack of copper, rhodonite
Self-centredness garnet
Self-confidence, lack of moss agate, copper, gold, rose quartz, ruby, sardonyx
Self-esteem, lack of lapis lazuli, malachite, turquoise
Sensitivity, lack of diamond, onyx, pearl, lapis lazuli, dark opal, ruby
Sexual problems lapis lazuli, dark opal, clear quartz, ruby
Shock diamond, pearl, ruby, Botswana agate, malachite
Shyness lapis lazuli
Speech problems apatite, amethyst
Suicidal gold, citrine
Superstition emerald, rose quartz, tiger's-eye
Uncertainty bloodstone, coral, diamond, emerald, peridot, malachite
Understanding, lack of malachite, dark pearl, tiger's-eye
Unforgiving nature rutile
Violent rose quartz, clear quartz, aquamarine
Will-power, lack of pink tourmaline, amethyst, garnet, carbon steel
Worry coral, topaz

I am indebted to David Lovell, of Crystal World, for his kind assistance in compiling the above information on gem elixirs. If you are interested in obtaining gem elixirs for yourself or would like to receive further information about gem elixirs, please write to:

David Lovell, Crystal World, 9, Cresswell Drive, Ravenstone, Leics, LE6 2AG

17

Crystal Miscellany

Crystal Exercises

Take a piece of rose quartz — about 1 kilogram (2lb) in weight — and twist, fairly tightly, a length of copper wire around it, leaving at least 15 cm (6 inches) free at each end.

Place the rose quartz in front of you and take hold of the ends of the copper wire, a piece in each hand. Now relax. Quieten your mind and be still. After a few moments you will begin to feel a gentle power pulsating within your hands. This power or energy will steadily increase and will become very pleasant. You will experience a deep sense of elation and a wonderful inner joy.

Practice yoga or meditation for a period of at least one hour. Then lie on your back and place a quartz crystal upon your third eye *chakra*. You will feel relaxed and your mind will become receptive to the subtle vibrations emanating from the crystal.

Ask the crystal to reflect the answers from the truth within into your conscious awareness. Then allow your mind to become open to receive the answer, which may come in symbols, images, visions or direct knowledge.

Hold the terminated point of a clear quartz crystal up to your third eye *chakra* and visualise yourself as being calm, confident and spontaneously flowing with the situation. Project this thought into your quartz crystal and then sit down quietly, holding the crystal, as you mentally reaffirm to yourself the positive image you have created.

If you need to ask for an answer to a specific question, ask your question mentally and then place your clear, single-terminated quartz crystal to your third eye *chakra* and visualise the solution in your mind's eye.

If you need to send loving thoughts or prayers to another person, place your quartz crystal pointing from your heart *chakra*, visualise the desired result as strongly as you can and then project the image through your crystal to be received by the person for whom you are praying.

Try the following when you next have 'flu: hold your personal quartz crystal and visualise yellow light radiating through it. Then place your crystal in water and drink this water next day; one cup of water at two-hourly intervals. You will be amazed at the result!

Many of us are exposed to very harsh tap water in our homes. One solution to this problem is to place a quartz crystal in a large jug of water, leave for a couple of hours, and then drink instead of the usual tap water. You will soon appreciate the sparkling purity of your crystal water.

Shirley MacLaine places quartz crystal clusters in the four corners of her bathtub every time she takes a bath (a great idea for reaching the parts that other healing can't reach!). Why not try it for yourself? — it's wonderful!

Try this experiment and you may be surprised at the results: form a healing circle with some of your friends. Place the person who is to receive the healing in the centre of the circle. The other members of the group should place their quartz crystals on the floor in front of them.

Each member of the healing circle should simultaneously send their love and healing thoughts to their crystals and direct the crystals to pass on their healing energies to the person sitting in the middle of the circle. You should find that *all* the people sitting in the circle receive a considerable amount of healing energy, and feel a great deal better as a result.

The following technique is useful for emotional and sexual blockages: lie on the floor on your back and place one small quartz crystal on your throat. Holding a quartz crystal in each hand, place one quartz crystal on your solar plexus, one on each thigh, where it meets the trunk, and one on your heart *chakra*. Breathe through your mouth seven times, in a steady rhythmic manner. As you inhale, slowly 'pull' energy from your heart into your throat, then gently, as you exhale, 'push' energy into the base *chakra* from your throat.

If this technique causes an emotional response, allow it to happen, and another block will have been removed.

Crystal Properties

Quartz crystals have many interesting qualities apart from its visual attractiveness. It can produce an electric current when put under tension or pressure and when it is influenced by an electric field it will vibrate rapidly at frequencies measured in millions per second. It is therefore used in resonators and oscillators for frequency control in electronic communications equipment. Quartz crystals also have the ability to transmit and amplify electro-magnetic energy. For this reason, quartz is used extensively in the field of electronics. More-over, it can also be used by you to tune into the deeper parts of yourself, because the parts of you which are not visible (e.g. your thoughts and your aura) consist of electro-magnetic energy.

It is not absolutely essential for you to believe, or understand, the power of the crystal for it to help you. But if you make an effort to work with your crystal, you can receive many benefits.

Hold your crystal as often as possible. The warmth of your body heats the crystal and excites the molecules, thereby intensifying the crystal's effectiveness.

Drinking crystal water increases and balances your energy field. Make pure crystal water by placing a crystal in a glass container, adding distilled or spring water, and setting it in the sun for a minimum of six hours. Try using a gallon jar.

A glass of crystal water, drunk with every meal, should be sufficient. More than that could cause over-stimulation. You should take a glass of crystal water before and after a massage, osteopathic session or any other healing or therapeutic treatment, to help integrate your energies. Heating or cooling the crystal water affects the energy level, so keep it at room temperature and use discretion with it when taking other forms of medication.

Plants respond very quickly to the flow of crystal energy. If you have a sick or ailing plant, try the following experiment. Pick up your personal quartz crystal and mentally programme the energies of the crystal to energise the plant. Then direct the single-terminated end of the crystal in a clockwise direction around the plant to strengthen its biomagnetic field. Do this several times. Now direct the crystal's energies towards the roots of the plant and visualise a ray of blue-white light pulsating towards the plant. When you have finished — and you will know when to stop intuitively — direct the crystal energies around the perimeter of the plant (once more) in a clockwise direction. Monitor the results carefully. The above treatment should be repeated at least once per day.

On one occasion I was staying with a family the night before I was to do a crystal healing workshop. In the evening I demonstrated my crystal wand techniques on my hostess. In the corner, behind the chair where she was sitting, was a Swiss cheese plant. When I arrived back home from giving the workshop I received an excited telephone call from the lady to tell me that her cheese plant had grown a further 15 cm (6 inches) during the night! And she sent me photographs to prove it. The cheese plant was now touching the ceiling.

Quartz crystals have a way of attracting children, who seem to be especially receptive to their beauty. A crystal hanging in a child's bedroom can become an endless source of fascination and delight.

Crystals or gemstones may be placed under the pillow during sleep to inspire lofty or prophetic dreams.

Hanging in a sunny window a quartz crystal will act as a prism, filling your room with brilliant spectrums and adding the radiance of colour and light to your surroundings. If the crystal is set gently in motion your room will sparkle with excitement and life as rainbows dance across the walls, floors and the ceiling.

18

Crystals and Headaches

Headaches deserve a special chapter of their own, because they are among the most common causes of discomfort that exist today. Few of us can boast that we are not susceptible to headaches or migraine from time to time. (Frequently people complain of having acquired a headache whilst participating in one of my crystal healing workshops or seminars, which is not really very surprising. At all my workshops and seminars I bring along with me hundreds of quartz crystals and gemstones, creating between them a tremendous amount of energy and power. The average person is not able to cope with the sudden overload of energy, with the result that headaches occur.)

When suffering from headaches or migraine try to avoid taking pain-killers in the form of aspirin or paracetamol. Pain-killers can actually interfere with the healing process by blocking the nerve endings so that the signal from the cells never gets to the brain. Since the brain does not know the cells are in trouble, it does not send the energy needed and the condition of the cells may worsen.

With our quartz crystals we can feed energy to the cells instead of blocking the pain signal so that the cells can repair themselves. This is the natural way of healing with crystals.

Energy flows in and out of the head all the time through the head and third eye *chakra*s. When a blockage, usually emotional or stressful, occurs at the mouth of the *chakra*, it builds up pressure. The excess pressure causes the cells to signal the brain with pain.

To treat a headache caused by stress, place your healing crystal in your right hand. Put your left hand over the site of the pain and the right hand over the solar plexus. Using the drawing ability of your left hand, amplified by the crystal in your right hand, now transfer the excess energy from your head to your solar plexus, where it can be distributed throughout the body. This may take up to 30 minutes to achieve. However, if you wish to speed up the healing process, close your eyes and picture the headache as a dark cloud of excess energy. Your left hand is a giant vacuum cleaner; watch it suck the cloud away. Watch closely until the cloud has all gone and then open your eyes. Put your hands down and stand up. Take a couple of deep breaths, walk around and wonder where your headache has gone!

At my workshops and seminars I can usually remove a headache by picking up my personal quartz crystal, directing the single-terminated end towards the person's head and slowly moving the crystal in a clockwise direction around the perimeter of the head. This can remove the headache completely within a couple of minutes.

19

Yoga and Crystals

I am indebted to Ambika Ife, a qualified yoga therapist and teacher of many years' experience for this chapter. Intuitively Ambika felt that she would be able to use the inner knowledge of crystals and gemstones to enhance and enrich the work that she was already doing in her yoga teaching.

Most of Ambika's work with crystals has been in conjunction with Hatha Yoga postures which she prescribes for people visiting her Venkatesa Yoga Centre. She has found that crystals and gemstones are a natural and powerful way of enhancing the benefits derived from the yoga postures. During her work Ambika has developed a number of very interesting crystal and gemstone configurations which are described below.

However, before discussing the actual configurations and their purposes it is necessary to give a brief explanation of Hatha Yoga and also provide a brief history of the relationship between crystals and yoga. This will help you to understand how these two excellent disciplines (each of which works very well on its own) can support one another.

Krishna (a divine incarnation of the Indian god Vishnu) proclaimed to his disciple Arjuna, 'All that you see and all that you cannot see is pervaded by a small part of me.' Krishna disclaims the idea of empty, meaningless space: God is everywhere, in everything, even in the space that separates us from each other. Out of this philosophy many methods of healing developed, each based on the existence of energy at several levels, not exclusively at the manifest level. Human beings also consist of subtle energies that are not manifest to the 'veiled' eye. The *Bhagavad Gita* describes an inverted tree with its roots above and its branches below; consciousness, which is above, polarised as *prana*, pours down to every part of the body. This balanced consciousness or *prana*, which animates the millions of cells of the body, is known as the subtle body. In it there are 72,000 *nadi*s (conduits, vessels, veins or nerves). The ancient Yogis or teachers explained in careful detail the construction of the subtle bodies and by what methods the subtle energies could be assessed.

The ultimate goal of all creation for the Hindu is the individual seeking God and then discovering that, in truth, nothing else exists, and that this body is only a microcosm of the great macrocosm of creation. Because the macrocosm is inaccessible the Yogi concentrates his efforts on the microcosm, the body.

One of the greatest methods of discovering the body was the use of a discipline that became known as *Hatha* yoga (*ha* = sun and *tha* = moon). In all the texts on Hatha Yoga, great attention is given to *Purusa*, the great One, the motionless, the contemplative, and to *Prakrti*, the One that works, that generates, that nourishes. These are said to be God and the manifest universe. But the texts warn us that this is a separation for the mind only — in truth they are both one! In the human body *Purusa* sits at the crown of the head, silent and uninvolved in the creation of the being, and *Prakrti* lies dormant at the base of the spine. Through the process of Hatha Yoga the being (which includes the subtle and gross body, the mind and the emotions) is purified and *Sakti*, in the form of the *Kundalini*, is awakened and united with *Purusa*. In order for this union to take place *Kundalini* must travel up a channel (or *nadi*) known as *Sushumna*. This central *nadi*, *Sushumna*, links the subtle body (corresponding to the position of the spine) to the crown of the head. In so doing it passes through a number of *chakras*. A *chakra* is a psychic centre of energy located at several places along *Sushumna*, each one of which is a mandala, pictured as a lotus flower with several petals.

Each mandala is associated with a cosmic element — earth, fire, air or space — and therefore bears the symbol of that element. Their locations in the subtle body are significant. The earth *chakra* is where the body comes into contact with the earth, the water *chakra* is in the genito-urinary region, the fire *chakra* is in the region of gastric fire, the air *chakra* is in the heart/lung region and the space *chakra* is in the throat (space is the medium of sound which is produced in the throat). Every centre has dual potentiality: the divine and the animal.

In the human personality each one of the elements manifests as a personality trait which has a dual aspect. The earth element imparts solidity and stabililty to the individual, but also stubbornness and earthiness. The water element imparts adaptability and clarity, but also instability and total lack of determination (water always takes the line of least resistance).

Hatha Yoga seeks to purify first and then to stabilise the energy centres in order that *Kundalini* can be awakened and begin her journey up *Sushumna*. The texts repeatedly emphasise that these purifications are of the greatest value to the Yogi's health. It is for this reason that Hatha Yoga may be viewed as a healing discipline because any disturbance in any of the *nadis* in the subtle body, or in the *chakras* themselves will have an immediate effect on the physical body.

If crystals and gemstones can also be used to stabilise and influence subtle energies then their effectiveness will be even greater when used in conjunction with other disciplines like Hatha Yoga. Other healing arts such as acupuncture and homoeopathy also seek to influence the subtle energies but in Hatha Yoga we are working with the manifest physical body and it seems more appropriate to influence the subtle energies using another manifest phsycial body, like a crystal.

Configurations to Purify *Sushumna, Pingala* and *Ida*

We could say that the vital energy, in the form of *prana*, circulates through the *nadis* and that the cosmic energy exists in a latent state in the *chakras*. Among the many *nadis*, 72 are of particular importance, but the most important, playing an essential role in all yogic techniques, are the first three: *Ida, Pingala* and *Sushumna. Sushumna* is referred to in many texts as the Great Way because it is up the *Sushumna* that *Kundalini* travels to the *chakras*.

All three of these *nadis* have their beginning at the perineum and *Ida* and *Pingala* travel up the body ending at the top of the left and right nostrils. However, they do not travel straight but spiral up the subtle body, going through the *chakras*. It is essential that these *nadis* are kept clear which is achieved through a recommended diet, exercise and adopting a conducive way of life, etc. Using both crystals and Hatha Yoga techniques we have devised the following methods for assisting in clearing the *nadis*:

1) (See Figures 8 and 9.) The patient is seated in a cross-legged position, the lotus position if possible. A clear quartz crystal is placed in the left hand pointing inward and one in the right hand pointing outward.

Figure 8

Figure 9

Two large quartz crystals are placed on the ground pointing towards the centre of the body (one at the front and one at the back). Four smaller crystals are placed on either side of the large crystal at the front of the patient's body. This posture should be held for 15 minutes, during which time the patient should do some form of *pranayama* (energy control through breathing) and visualisation. The release from the posture must be slow, controlled and focused and should take approximately 4 minutes.

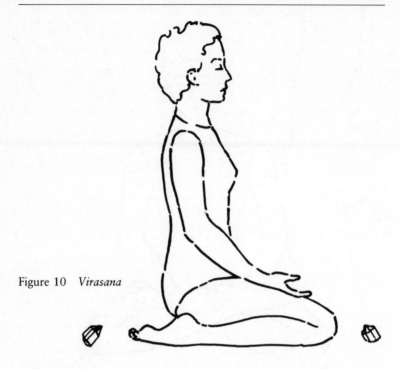

Figure 10   *Virasana*

2) (See Figure 10.) The patient assumes *virasana* (*vira* means a hero). The quartz crystals are placed on the ground in the same configuration as (1) above but this time, instead of holding crystals in the palm of the hands, they are placed on the wrists using wrist straps. The crystal on the left wrist points inward and the crystal on the right wrist points outward. This posture should also be held for 15 minutes during which time specific *pranayama* exercises are done, and then released slowly during the final 4 minutes.

3) People who have been practising postures (1) and (2) for some time should then proceed to *sury namaskar* (salute to the sun) (Figure 11). During *sury namaskar* one large quartz crystal is placed in front of the body, and one behind. The crystal wrist straps are put on and so is a forehead strap with a clear quartz crystal pointing upwards. During this posture the patient is required to keep the crystal in front of the body directed to the centre of the body.

Figure 11
Sury namaskar

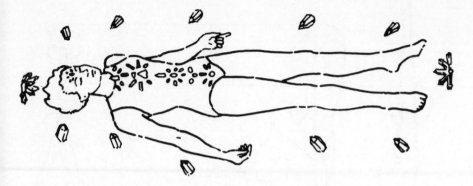

Figure 12   *Savasana* (the pose of the dead body)

Configurations to balance *chakras*

The patient should lie down in *savasana* (the pose of the dead body; see Figure 12). The crystals and gemstones are then placed on the body at each *chakra* point as follows: at *muladhara chakra*, which is located at the mouth of the *Sushumna*, below the genitals and just above the anus (Figure 13);

Figure 13

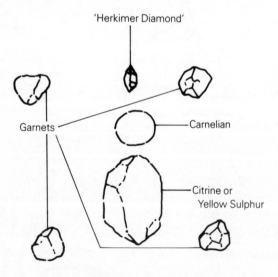

at *anahata* (heart) *chakra*, in the centre of the heart region (Figure 14); at

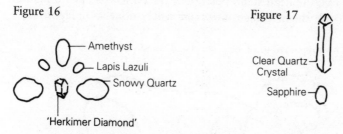

Figure 14

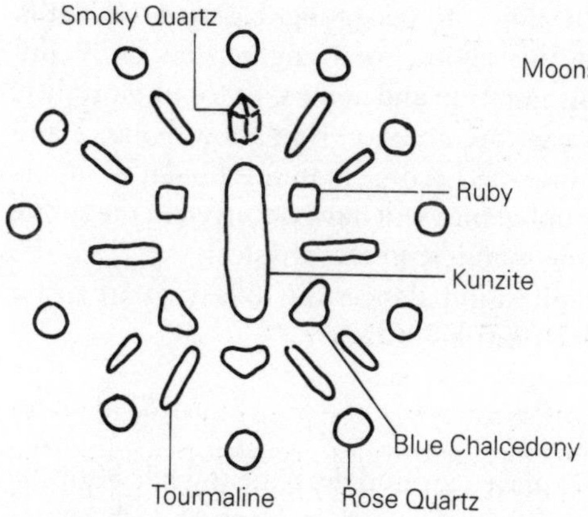

Smoky Quartz

Ruby

Kunzite

Blue Chalcedony

Tourmaline   Rose Quartz

Figure 15

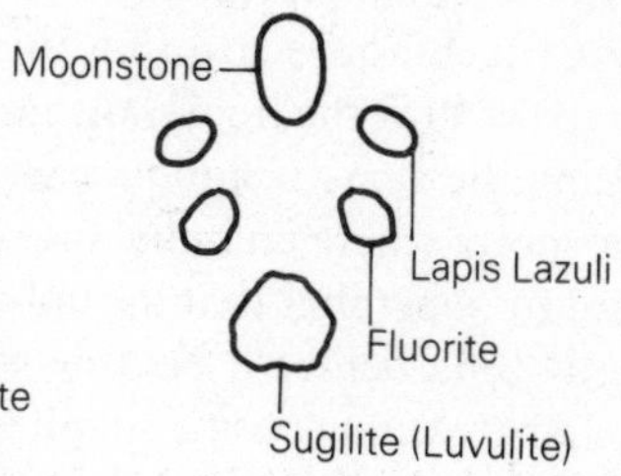

Moonstone

Lapis Lazuli

Fluorite

Sugilite (Luvulite)

visuddha (throat) *chakra*, situated at the base of the throat (Figure 15); at *ajna* (third eye) *chakra*, in the centre of the forehead (Figure 16); at *sahasrara* (head) *chakra*, at the crown of the head (the crystals are placed on

Figure 16

Amethyst

Lapis Lazuli

Snowy Quartz

'Herkimer Diamond'

Figure 17

Clear Quartz Crystal

Sapphire

the floor, resting against the head) (Figure 17).

Around the body are then placed twelve quartz crystals (as in Figure 12), all pointing upward, towards the head of the patient.

It is rarely necessary to do a full *chakra* layout. Usually, if there is a specific health problem, in the kidneys, for example, Ambika will do a *muladhara* layout only. Or, if there is a heart complaint, she will do a layout on both the heart, *anahata chakra*, and on the *svadhisthana chakra*.

Configurations for Specific Imbalances

The great Yogi Vajrayana was directed to obtain a 'body of diamond', incorruptible, not subject to becoming. He used the Hatha Yoga techniques to bring this about, to strengthen his body and prepare it for the final transmutation and make it fit for immortality. Using the same techniques we are able to bring about balance and harmony where an imbalance has become manifest (and it is important to remember that the imbalance will have occurred in the subtle body long before it became manifest in the physical).

For treating specific manifest imbalances the following are just a few of the techniques which can be of use:

Anaemia

Six large quartz crystals are placed around the patient while he or she is practising the posture routines. Directly in front of each quartz crystal there should be a green tourmaline wand. These stay in position all through the session. The Hatha Yoga routine would include:

1 *Sirasana*, the head stand posture (if the patient is new to Hatha Yoga only the first stage of *sirasana* will be done, as in Figure 18).

Figure 18 Preparation for *sirasana* (head stand posture)

Figure 20 *Sarvangasana*
(shoulder stand)

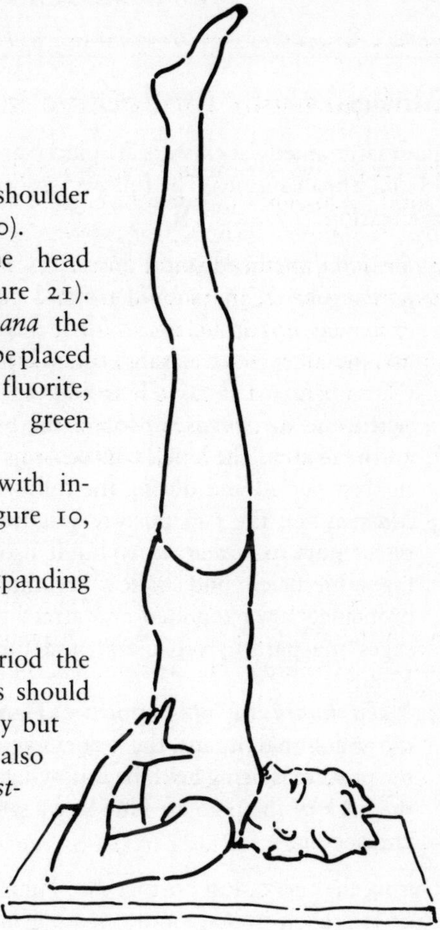

2 *Sarvangasana*, the shoulder stand posture (Figure 20).

3 *Paschimottanasana*, the head to knees posture (Figure 21). During *paschimottanasana* the following stones would be placed on the back: red coral, fluorite, garnet, black and green tourmaline.

4 *Uttanasana*, extended with intensity posture (see Figure 10, p. 116).

5 *Ujjayi pranayama*, an expanding *pranayama* exercise.

During the relaxation period the normal relaxation crystals should be placed around the body but gemstone layouts should also be placed on the *svadhisthana* and *anahata chakras* (see Figure 12, p. 118).

Figure 21
Paschimottanasana
(forward bend)

Asthma

Four large amethyst clusters are placed around the patient during the Hatha Yoga routines. The following postures should be included in the session:

1 *Sirasana*, the head stand posture (see Figure 19).

2 *Sarvangasana*, the shoulder stand posture (see Figure 20); an extremely important *asana* for the asthmatic. Before the patient assumes the posture, a small round lapis lazuli should be placed at the base of the throat. This adds to the purifying effect of the posture as *sarvangasana* forces the *prana* into the chest, throat and head area. The lapis lazuli remains at the throat *chakra* during the rest period and during the following posture.

3 *Matsyasana*, the fish posture (Figure 22). *Matsyasana* is complementary to *sarvangasana* but it also has its own unique advantages. Inefficient and shallow breathing is corrected as the upper bronchials are expanded and stretched. This posture also massages the parathyroid gland and the all-important suprarenal glands.

4 *Maha mudra*, the noble posture (Figure 23). This posture tones the abdominal organs, the kidneys and the adrenal glands. While the posture is being held the following stones should be placed on the back of the patient; blue lace agate (over the lung area), and chrysocolla.

During the relaxation posture (see Figure 12, p. 118) the amethyst clusters are left in place and gemstone layouts should be done over the *muladhara, anahata* and *visuddha chakras* (see pp. 124–30).

During relaxation the patient should assume *savasana* (see Figure 15) during which period it is possible to place various configurations around and on the body at the various *chakra* centres. The relaxation can therefore be heightened and various problems helped and eased. For example, people suffering from sinus complaints and nasal catarrh always benefit from having lapis lazuli placed on their forehead during the relaxation period.

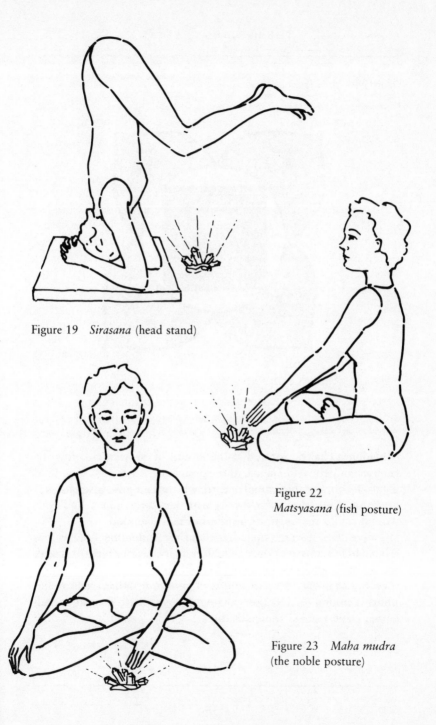

Figure 19   *Sirasana* (head stand)

Figure 22
Matsyasana (fish posture)

Figure 23   *Maha mudra*
(the noble posture)

Figure 24   *Muladhara chakra*

Muladhara chakra: located at the mouth of *Sushumna* below the genitals and above the anus, in the perineum. It has four blood red petals. It contains the symbol of earth which is the yellow square. It is here that *Kundalini-Sakti* dwells with her three and a half coils wound round the *linga*, its head a brilliant diamond.

This *chakra* governs the adrenals in the endocrine system. It is related to the cohesive power of matter, to inertia, the birth of sound, the sense of smell, the outgoing breath.

Stones that may be used in a configuration: citrine; yellow sulphur; diamond (or Herkimer diamond); garnets; red coral; bloodstone; jasper; onyx; rhodochrosite.

Figure 25 *Svadhisthana chakra*

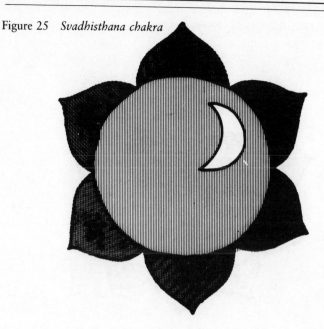

Svadhisthana chakra: this centre is in the region of the genitals. It has six petals of vermilion colour. It contains the water symbol (which is white) in its centre. In the middle is a white crescent moon.

This *chakra* governs the gonads and is related to the ingoing breath. It governs the sense of taste and controls the extremities, i.e. hands and feet.

Stones that may be used in a configuration: kyanite; moonstone; topaz; green tourmaline; aquamarine; red coral; jasper; loadstone; bloodstone; magnetite.

Figure 26   *Manipura chakra*

Manipura chakra: located in the navel region. Its 10 petals are the dark blue colour of the rain cloud. It is the fire sign, and contains a radiant triangle the colour of the rising sun. Within the triangle is the fire symbol.

This *chakra* governs the pancreas, the menstrual flow, the sense of sight and the digestive breath.

Stones that may be used in a configuration: orpiment; ruby; agate; topaz; lapis lazuli; sodalite; copper; amber; blue tourmaline.

Figure 27   *Anahata chakra*

Anahata chakra: the centre of the heart region. Its 12 petals are of a red/gold colour. In its centre is a smoky star: the air symbol. At this region we find the radiance of 'ten million lightning flashes'. It is the place where the individual soul (*jiva*) resides. This is also the region of sound without contact between two objects.

This *chakra* governs the thymus, the sense of touch, potency, the motor forces, and the blood system.

Stones that may be used in a configuration: rose quartz; blue and green tourmaline; ruby; gold; picture agate; blue chalcedony; kunzite; smoky quartz; red coral; malachite; azurite; eilat stone.

Figure 28   *Visuddha chakra*

Visuddha chakra: this centre is situated at the base of the throat. It has 16 purple petals. In the pericarp is the space (*akash*) sign, within which is the full moon. It is the link between *ajna* and *anahata* (the head and the heart).

This *chakra* governs the thyroid and parathyroid. It governs *udana* (the vital air that fills the body), and the skin.

Stones that can be used in a configuration: moonstone; blue chalcedony; lapis lazuli; fluorite; gold; royal lazel (sugilite).

Figure 29   *Ajna chakra*

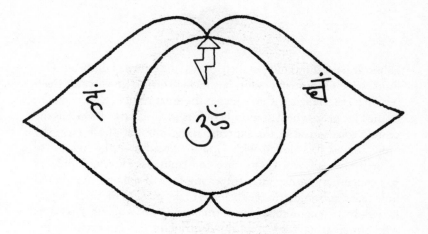

Ajna chakra: located in the centre of the forehead. All three *nadis* —
sushumna, ida and *pingala* meet here and end here. It is white and has
two white petals. At the top is a triangle pointing upward from which
comes a lightning flash. Above this is a luminosity and everything
from *muladhara* upwards is visible — right up to the crown of the
head. In the *ajna chakra* is the sacred monosyllable '*om*'. It is in this
centre that the meditator has the vision of God.

This *chakra* controls the pituitary and pineal glands and the
hypothalamus. It is the seat of cognitive faculties and the senses in
their 'subtle' form. Near *ajna chakra* is the *karana-rupa* — seat of the
seven 'causal forms' which are held to produce and maintain the
subtle and the physical bodies.

Stones that can be used in a configuration: snow quartz; diamond
(or Herkimer diamond); amethyst; lapis lazuli.

Figure 30 *Sahasrara*

Sahasrara: the thousand-petalled lotus at the crown of the head. This lotus, which is pure in colour, has its face turned downward. Deep within it is a triangle within which is the great void. In it is the *bindu*, or the blue pearl which grants liberation, in the centre of which is the cosmic consciousness, the supreme being, the self of all. Here the individual soul is united with God — *cit-sakti* — the union. All diversity is reabsorbed into pure consciousness energy, *Kundalini* has ended her journey after traversing the six *chakras*. We should note that *sahasrara* no longer belongs to the plane of the body — that it already designates the plane of transcendence — and this explains why writers usually speak of the doctrine of six *chakras*.

Stones that can be used in configuration: sapphire; clear quartz crystal.

APPENDIX I

Case Histories

In setting out the following, grateful thanks and acknowledgement must go to all those people who contributed their experiences. It is very encouraging that more and more healers are now using crystals and gemstones in their own clinical practice.

Henry, the Crystallised Cat

One Sunday morning, Wendy found her lovely cat lying in the road outside her home, having been run over by a car.

Henry was still alive but obviously in a very bad way. It appeared that his spine had been broken, so he was taken immediately to the vet, to be put down. The vet said that it wasn't his spine that was the problem, but his pelvis, which was broken in three places.

Henry could be saved, but it would be a very long job involving several months' care. Wendy decided to take a chance on Henry eventually recovering, and so took him back home and placed him in a special cage to keep him perfectly still. She also hung the quartz crystal I had given her for Christmas on Henry's cage. The vet wanted to see Henry again after a period of 10 days, when he explained that it would be many weeks before he could possibly be back on his feet.

Henry was progressing quite well with no setbacks, so the next visit was scheduled for a date four weeks after the accident. When Henry attended the vet on this occasion, he was on his feet and walking about on the surgery table — in front of a totally astonished vet, who kept saying: 'But he can't be on his feet yet!'

The following week, Henry was taken to the vet again (five weeks after the accident). This time he was on the floor trying to climb up the leg of the surgery table, whereupon two vets examined him and even took another set of X-rays to establish that he really had broken his pelvis in three places, and there and then he was discharged as completely fit. Henry left the vet's surgery in triumph, leaving behind two very perplexed vets.

. . . Which is why he is now known as 'Henry, the Crystallised Cat'.

A Healing Effect

A young man was attending the hospital with a very painful abscess under his arm. It was being treated with antibiotics by a doctor and had been lanced, but it was not healing very well. To assist the healing process, crystal healing was tried by his natural health practitioner. First the therapist pointed a single-terminated quartz crystal at the wound and, in addition, used an orange-coloured gel on the crystal light box.

The patient was very pleased to report that when he next visited his doctor the wound had healed completely and all the inflammation had completely disappeared!

The Jade Pendant

The following letter is typical of many that I have received after despatching an appropriate crystal pendant for healing purposes.

'Thank you for my pendant, and may I relate a funny "coincidence" about the Jade? The morning after I sent off to you for my pendant I awoke with the name "Jade" in my mind. I pushed it aside and thought no more about it.

Then your pendant arrived and, imagine my surprise, when it turned out to be a Jade pendant? Curious, or what?

Thus far I have this to relate about the "effect" since wearing the said Jade pendant. For weeks I have been plagued by back pains and problems with my bladder and bowels. I had tried a few things, and then decided that it had come on its own, and it will subside likewise, as I do not believe in too much doctoring of oneself; you may do more harm than good!

However, twenty-four hours after wearing your Jade pendant, my how the water flowed, and the back ache ceased. Further, the whites of my eyes have cleared and I am sleeping better and not disturbed with the night "loo" visits — so I leave it with you . . . '

The Spiritual Healer

Kaushal Gupta, a family doctor aged 50, was declared bankrupt with very substantial debts following the failure of a number of business dealings completely unrelated to his medical career.

As a result he relinquished his former medical practice and set up a spiritual healing clinic alongside his new, private, medical practice. He claims to have treated some 150 people in a 9-month period, using the combined techniques of crystal healing and laying-on of hands healing with notable successes:

I have been flabbergasted at what I have seen. All right, people say, you use crystals but since you are a healer as well, how can you evaluate your results and say that this healing — or cure — was as a result of you using crystals? Or that this healing was because of you as a healer? Quite rightly, you can't. I learnt about healing before I learnt about crystals and I don't differentiate between ordinary healing and crystal healing. I can't really be bothered! Let some one else work it out if they can!

A retired miner, aged about 57 or 58 years old, came to me with a frozen shoulder; a frozen shoulder to such a degree that he couldn't move his shoulder more than about 15–20 degrees.

He was in a great deal of pain. On his right side, also, he suffered from tennis elbow and that was equally painful. I said to him, 'Would you let me try some healing on you?' Most of my patients do know that I indulge in various forms of healing in addition to my medical practice. I don't normally prescribe medicines and I don't particularly want to do so. Not unless a patient actually pleads with me to prescribe something . . .

So he hummed and hawed and eventually said yes, he would let me have a go.

I let him hold two of my quartz crystals whilst I laid my hands on his back for about 10 minutes. Having done the healing I forgot all about it.

I went back to him three weeks later. It was a house visit. I went in to see him and he made me a cup of tea. I asked him, 'Shall I do a bit more?'

He said, 'More of what?'

'Healing for your shoulder,' I said.

I couldn't believe what I saw. He raised his arms up into the air and then bent his elbows fully. He said that he was 100 per cent free! I was amazed: I would not have expected his tennis elbow or frozen shoulder to have improved so quickly by more than 40 per cent from having received any known allopathic treatment.

A boy of 14 spent a few days in hospital with pain on the right side of his stomach. His parents called me in. I went and saw the lad and gave him a full medical examination. I said, 'Whatever it is, it is not his appendix. You cannot have appendicitis for seven days'. (Which was the duration of the pain.)

I made completely sure in my own mind that it was not a surgical problem. As usual I gave him my two quartz crystals to hold in his hands. I placed my hands on the front and back of his stomach area. I didn't expect anything. After about 5 minutes I said, 'Let me have the crystals back and now stand up for me, walk to the door, take a couple of steps and then come back to me and lie down again. Now then, how's your pain?'

He said: 'I have no pain!'

'You have no pain! Tell me how long did you actually have the pain before I saw you today?'

'Oh,' he said, 'seven days'.

Now I thought that was a miracle!

A woman of 85 had had chest pains for three weeks. I checked her blood pressure and found no evidence of pleurisy. All I could say medically was that there was nothing disastrously wrong with her. So I gave her my two quartz crystals, showed her my healing card, and explained what I was about to do. I placed my hands on the front and back of her chest and after about 5–6 minutes I took the crystals back.

I asked her to take a couple of deep breaths, which she did. Then I asked her how her pain was. She told me that she had no pain! I was so surprised that I had to check my facts again. She had had her pain for three weeks and now she had no pain whatsoever!

The very same day, a woman of 74, who had been suffering from dizzy spells for the previous three or four weeks, received a house visit from me.

Her blood pressure was all right and I examined her to make sure that medically everything was as good as it could be. She also told me that her vision, in her right eye, had become blurred.

I gave her my two quartz crystals to hold and told her what I was going to do. I put one hand over the eye which was blurred for about 5–6 minutes. 'Now then,' I said, 'how is your eyesight now?'

She blinked once or twice and then said, 'You know, Doctor, I think I can see a little better now than before my vision had started to become blurred!' I said that I wasn't really surprised, though, in all truth, I was most surprised!

And her dizziness had improved to such an extent that she was able to go to the kitchen and make me a cup of coffee and bring it to me without spilling a drop!

The lady lived in sheltered housing accommodation and just then the warden walked in. I said to the warden, 'She has just walked into her kitchen, made me a cup of coffee and brought it back to me without spilling a drop; and she's supposed to be dizzy!' The warden couldn't believe it either.

Other patients who have received relief at the hands of Dr Gupta include an 80-year-old man with lung cancer, given only a few months to live, who was completely stabilised after treatment. A 44-year-old musician visibly improved despite having inoperable lung cancer and a man in constant pain following an abdominal valve transplant for a circulation disorder reported relief after experiencing intense heat as Dr Gupta laid his hands on the affected area.

A Crystal Healing
Learning Programme

Whilst crystal healing may not be a new therapy, it is new to the twentieth century. Other major, and well-established, therapies in the field of natural health such as massage, osteopathy, homoeopathy, herbalism, aromatherapy, reflexology and hypnotherapy have taken a very long time to become respected and accepted. Credibility — in the eyes of the general public and one's fellow natural health practitioners — often depends very much on attaining an appropriate qualification and certificate.

Unfortunately, there are many organisations, on both sides of the Atlantic, who offer bogus certificates in many different subjects, including those in the area of natural health. These certificates are not worth the paper they are printed on.

Any form of healing — whether it be crystal healing or any other type of healing — can be very difficult to examine. Many of the finest healers throughout the world possess a wonderful healing gift which would be impossible to examine. However, as Director of the Crystal Research Foundation, I decided that we should make some efforts to place crystal healing in a position where it would become fully accepted and understood as a major therapy. Anthony Baird, Director of the Institute of Complementary Medicine in London was most helpful, providing invaluable advice and ideas on how a learning course should be formulated.

The purpose of the course programme is to enable people of all age groups to use the knowledge and techniques of crystal healing for private or professional use. It is based upon six, non-residential, weekends — Course A and Course B (three weekends each). The final weekend of both includes a three-hour written examination and a two-hour practical examination. Students are required to have passed the written and practical examinations for Course A before progressing to Course B.

Participants need to have obtained a minimum number of crystals and gemstones before the end of the second weekend.

Syllabus for Course A includes:

Weekend 1

1 Crystals through the Ages
2 The Healing Properties of Stones
3 Healing with Crystals — Choosing, Cleansing, Dedicating, Programming
4 Vibrations and Energies
5 The Crystal Kingdom
6 Dowsing with Crystals
7 Crystal Numerology
8 Aura-scanning
9 Self-healing through Crystals
10 The Astrological Significance of Stones — Birth Stones
11 Crystal Wands
12 Pyramids

The above provides a basic understanding of the use of crystals for the purpose of healing.

A crystal light box is needed for this weekend.

Weekend 2

1 Colour Crystal Healing
2 The *Chakras*
3 The Thymus
4 Electro-crystal therapy
5 Crystal Sound Therapy
6 Crystal Configurations
7 Crystal Potions
8 Gem Remedies
9 Yoga and Crystals

Weekend 3

1 Advanced Crystal Configurations
2 Crystal Massage
3 The Total Healing Experience (Colour, Sound and Crystals)
4 Crystal Patterns
5 Experimentation

Written and practical examinations take place at the end of this weekend. Course B (a further three weekends) does not commence until at least three months after the final weekend of Course A.

Before the first weekend of Course B participants should have completed a 5,000 word thesis based upon information provided at the end of Course A.

The syllabus for Course B has to be ever-changing, with the opportunity of further experimentation in many different aspects of crystal healing. Encouragement of lateral thinking is very important, as is an active contribution to the course.

In summary, such a learning programme aims to:

1 increase awareness and acceptance, by practitioners and the public, of all aspects of crystal healing;
2 maintain and improve standards of practice by providing regular workshops, seminars and conferences;
3 encourage co-operation between registered medical practitioners and all organisations concerned with health and healing; and
4 promote research into crystal healing.

For further information about the Crystal Research Foundation and its Healing Certificated Course, please write to:

The Course Registrar,
The Crystal Research Foundation,
37, Bromley Road,
St Annes-on-Sea,
Lancashire,
England FY8 1PQ

Bibliography

Alper, Rev. Frank, *Exploring Atlantis* (Vols 1–3), Arizona Metaphysical Society, Phoenix, 1982–1985.

Anthology: *The Crystal Sourcebook*, Mystic Crystal Publications, 1987.

Baer, Randall and Vicki, *The Windows of Light*, Harper & Row, New York, 1984.

The Crystal Connection, Harper & Row, New York, 1987.

Berlitz, Charles, *Atlantis — the Lost Continent Revealed*, Fontana/Collins, London, 1984.

Bhattacharya, B., *Gem Therapy*, Firma KLM Ltd., Calcutta, 1957.

Bonewitz, Ra, *Cosmic Crystals*, Turnstone Press, Wellingborough, 1983.

The Cosmic Crystal Spiral, Element Books, Shaftesbury, Dorset, 1986.

Bryant, Page, *Crystals and Their Uses*, Sun Books, Santa Fe, New Mexico, 1984.

Cayce, Edgar, *Gems and Stones*, Association of Research and Enlightenment, Virginia Beach, 1979.

Edgar Cayce on Atlantis, Association of Research and Enlightenment, Virginia Beach, 1962.

Edgar Cayce on Reincarnation, Association of Research and Enlightenment, Virginia Beach, 1971.

Crow, W.B., *Precious Stones*, Aquarian, 1980.

Davidson, John, *Subtle Energy*, C.W. Daniels, Saffron Walden, 1986.

Deaver, Korra, *Rock Crystal*, Samuel Weiser, New York, 1985.

Gimbel, Theo, *Healing Through Colour*, C.W. Daniels, Saffron Walden, 1980.
Form, Sound, Colour and Healing, C.W. Daniels, Saffron Walden, 1987.
Gurudas, *Gem Elixirs and Vibrational Healing* (Vols 1 & 2), Cassandra Press, Boulder, 1985 & 1986.
Kilner, W.J., *The Aura*, Samuel Weiser, New York, 1973.
Kunz, George, *The Curious Lore of Precious Stones*, Dover, New York, 1971.
Markham, Ursula, *Fortune Telling by Crystals*, Aquarian, Wellingborough Press, 1987.
Nielsen, Greg and Thoth, Max, *Pyramid Power*, Warner Books, New York, 1976.
Raphaell, Katrina, *Crystal Enlightenment*, Aurora Press, New York, 1985.
Crystal Healing, Aurora Press, New York, 1987.
Rolfe, Mona, *Initiation by the Nile*, C.W. Daniels, Saffron Walden, 1976.
Smith, Michael, *Crystal Power*, Llewellyn Publications, St Paul, 1985.
Tansley, David, *Chakras, Rays and Radionics*, C.W. Daniels, Saffron Walden, 1984.
Ray Paths and Chakra Gateways, C.W. Daniels, Saffron Walden, 1985.
Uyldert, Mellie, *The Magic of Precious Stones*, Turnstone Press, Wellingborough, 1981.

USEFUL ADDRESSES

The following is a list of crystal healers, therapists, remedists, diagnosticians, advisors, teachers and suppliers who are involved in many aspects of crystal healing and associated therapy:

UK

Bishop, Barbara, M.I.A.T., M.Crys.H., Colour therapist and crystal healing therapist, 8 Woodcombe Cottages, Woodcombe, Minehead, Somerset TA24 8SE

Bodytreats Ltd. (aromatherapy oils), 15, Approach Road, Raynes Park, London SW20 8BA

Bovenizer, Suzanne, M.Crys.H., Westwood, Cronks Hill, Reigate, Surrey RH2 7EQ

Bright Star, 61, Theydon Street, Walthamstow, London E17 8EW

Collins, Gillian, The Secretary, Association of Crystal Healing Therapists, 5 Sunnymede Valley, Holcombe Brook, Bury, Lancashire BL0 9RR

Collins, Marshall, 'Crystal Light' Healing Centre, 9, Station Road, Otley, Yorkshire LS21 3HX

Copperthwaite, Eric, 20, Harts Leap Road, Sandhurst, Camberley, Surrey GU17 8EW

Crowe, John, M.A. (Hum Psych), M.F. Phys, 10, Crossways Park, Howey, Llandrindod Well, Powys, Wales

The Editor, *Crystal News*, 37, Bromley Road, St Annes-on-Sea, Lancashire FY8 1PG

The Crystal Research Foundation, 37, Bromley Road, St Annes-on-Sea, Lancashire, FY8 1PQ

Crystal World, Anubis House, 9, Cresswell Drive, Ravenstone, Leics, LE6 2AG

Ford, Dr Helen, Holistic Health Centre, 119, Hagley Road, Stourbridge, West Midlands DY8 1RD

Gallagher, Brigid, M.Crys.H., 28, Alderbrook Terrace, Edinburgh, Scotland EH11 1TA

Gimbel, Theo, Brook House, Avening, Tetbury, Gloucestershire GL8 8NS

Ife, Ambika, M.Crys.H., 44, Grosvenor Road, Caversham, Reading, Berkshire RG4 0FN

Joyce, Judith, M.Crys.H., Meadow Cottage, Narkurs, Torpoint, Cornwall

Keyte, Geoffrey, M.Crys.H., 37, Bromley Road, St Annes-on-Sea, Lancashire FY8 1PQ

Oldfield, Harry, 117, Long Drive, South Ruislip, Middlesex HA4 0HL

Shambhala, 8, The Market Place, Glastonbury, Somerset

Simcock, Mary, D.O., 'The Gitty', 7–9, Noreth Square, Newport Pagnell, Buckinghamshire MK16 8EP

Smith, Robin, M.Crys.H., 1, Heaston Terrace, Millbrook, Torpoint, Cornwall PL10 1EF

Sneigon, Charles, Laureston House, 72, New Road, Brixham, Devon TQ5 8NJ

Spiritual Venturers Association, 72, Pasture Road, Goole, North Humberside DN14 6HE

Summerscales, Joanne, 79, Kings Road, South Harrow, Middlesex HA2 9JG

Torpoint Crystal Healing Centre, 3–4, Moor View, Torpoint, Cornwall PL11 2LH

West, Dennis, M.Crys.H., Crystal House, 4, Bridgewater Road, Bleadon, Weston-Super-Mare, Avon BS24 0BG

New Zealand

Allan, Gina MIC, IBA, Aotearoa Healing and Crystal Foundation, Sunhaven, c/o Bombay P.O., South Auckland

Australia

Ney, Michael, P.O. Box 566, Milson's Point, 2061, Sydney

USA

Alper, Dr Frank, Arizona Metaphysical Society, 3639, East Clarendon Road, Pheonix, AZ 85108

Badgley, Dr Laurence, 370, W.San Bruno, San Bruno, CA 94066

Bryant, Page, C/O Sun Publishing Co., P O Box 4383, Albuquerque, N M 87196

Diamond, Madina, 99–07, 43rd Avenue, Corona, New York, NY 11368

Flanagan, Gael Crystal, P O Box 2285, Sedona, AZ 86336

Nocerino, Nick, Crystal Skull Society International, P O Box 302, Pinole, CA 94564

Schepper, Richard, 185–01, Hillside Avenue, Jamaica, NY 11432

Silbey, Uma, P O Box 31131, San Francisco, CA 94131

Smith, Michael, M G S Communications, P O Box 26881, Lakewood, CO 80226

Vogel, Dr Marcel, Psychic Research Inc, 17235, Little Orchard Street, San Jose, CA 95125

Walker, Dael, The Crystal Company, P O Box 348, Sunol, CA 94586

West Germany

Chockron, Daya Sarai, Adalbert Strasse, 10, Rg1, 8000, Munich 40

INDEX

Please note: page numbers in *italics* refer to pages on which illustrations appear.